STYLE

SECOND EDITION

Ten Lessons

in

Clarity

&

Grace

STYLE

SECOND EDITION

Ten Lessons in Clarity & Grace

JOSEPH M. WILLIAMS
University of Chicago

SCOTT, FORESMAN AND COMPANY
Glenview, Illinois
London, England

Excerpt from *Notes of a Native Son* by James Baldwin, copyright
© 1955 by James Baldwin. Reprinted by permission of Beacon Press
and Michael Joseph Ltd.

D. H. Lawrence, *Studies in Classic American Literature*. New York:
The Viking Press, 1961.

Norman Mailer. *Armies of the Night*. New York: The New American
Library, Inc., 1971.

From *Science and the Common Understanding* by J. Robert Oppenheimer.
Copyright © 1954 by J. Robert Oppenheimer, renewed © 1981 by
Robert B. Meyner. Reprinted by permission of Simon & Schuster, Inc.

2 3 4 5 6–MVN–89 88 87 86 85

Library of Congress Cataloging in Publication Data

Williams, Joseph M.
  Style: ten lessons in clarity and grace.

  Includes index.
    1. English language—Rhetoric.   2. English language—Style.   3. English
language—Business English.   4. English language—Technical English.
I. Title.
PE1421.W545 1985   808'.042   84–13966
ISBN 0–673–18058–1

. . . English style, familiar but not coarse,
elegant but not ostentatious . . .

Samuel Johnson

To my mother and father

Preface

To Those Who Write on the Job

Fortunately, most of you require no convincing about the importance of a clear and readable style, especially if you have to waste a large part of your day struggling through the prose of those who have never learned to write well. Unfortunately, the advice that most of us recall about writing well probably doesn't help us correct even our own bad writing. If what we remember is typical of most such advice, it probably consists of banalities such as "Be clear, be concise," or of useless minutiae such as "Don't begin sentences with *and* or end them with prepositions."

The kind of confused writing that most of us have to live with fails for reasons that don't yield to well-meant but empty generalities or to any list of particular dos and don'ts. To understand why anyone—including ourselves—writes badly, we have to be able to look at a sentence and understand how it works, how the ideas have been distributed through its different parts, and then decide how to write it better.

To address that problem, we have to be specific and concrete, and that means we have to use some of those terms we may or may not remember from junior high school—*verb, object, noun, active, passive,* and so on. Every subject has a vocabulary which anyone learning that subject has to master. It's the same with style: If you want to understand and improve your own, you have to control a few terms. There aren't a lot of them here, they're not difficult, and every one of them is defined in the Appendix. Under no circumstances waste your time trying to memorize them. Simply learning how to define nouns and verbs won't help you write any better. But if you can develop a sense of how nouns and verbs differ, you'll understand what distinguishes good and bad writing, and *that* will help you write better.

Something I have found repeatedly among those who have a problem with the way people in their organization write is the lack of a common language about writing and its problems. If you are responsible for the writing of others and you find it unacceptable, you have to communicate to those writers more than your displeasure. You have to tell them what to do to write better. Yet time and again I have seen administrators simply ignore the problem because they don't feel confident discussing style: Neither the administrator nor the subordinate has a vocabulary to express what either sees as the source of the difficulty. Or if an administrator does try to explain what's wrong, his or her language is likely to be vague, impressionistic, and different from the language of others in the organization who must also tell their subordinates how to improve their writing.

This book provides the consistent and explicit vocabulary that will let you address a writing problem consistently and explicitly.

To Students

Nothing is more tedious than learning a skill that seems to have no immediate application and no obvious value, even in the distant future. You've already learned how to write well enough to get as far as you've come. And when you read all those textbooks, journal articles, and scholarly monographs written in language so turgid and incomprehensible that it sets one's head to throbbing, the penalty for bad writing must seem to be not especially severe. If someone can write badly and still get published, why should any of us spend the time and effort learning how to write well?

The answer is one that you will have to take partly on faith: First, and most obviously, the very scarcity of clear and precise writing makes it that much more valuable. Even though an unclear and imprecise style obviously does not bar a good many writers from getting into print, a person who can write clearly and gracefully goes out into the world with an uncommon skill. One important reason business people and professionals do not achieve what their potential might otherwise allow is their inability to communicate, to get their good ideas down on paper in a way that lets others understand those ideas quickly and easily. In every survey that asks business people what subjects they wish they had studied more carefully, their first or second answer is always communication.

True, you might compensate for a turgid style with great

ideas, with an original and creative mind. But the more common truth is that most of us have minds and ideas that are closer to merely good than to outstandingly brilliant. And ideas that are only good need all the help they can get. So if we weren't born brilliant, we can at least learn to be clear; it is, in fact, an ability that is just as rare as inherited genius, and most of the time considerably more useful.

I know how unpersuasive this kind of "let-me-tell-you-what's-good-for-you" argument is before you've tested it against hard experience. But in fact, you may already have conducted the test: How often have you wanted to toss aside a textbook or journal article whose every leaden sentence was an agony to read? How many sentences have you reread and reread again, struggling to extract whatever meaning may or may not have sunk under the weight of all that verbiage? How often have you read a dozen pages only to realize that you can't recall a single idea?

You have to read that kind of writing now, perhaps because it's been assigned, perhaps because you need it for a term paper. But suppose for a moment that you were the boss of someone who wrote badly, and that you've just received a memo or report written in that tangled, abstract style. What do you think would be your first impulse?

Finally, the tone of this book is strongly prescriptive. Its lessons will tell you in a straightforward way how to write clearly. I think the advice is sound. I've tested it with a good many adult writers in government, the professions, and business. So far, no one has objected that the problems we will be addressing are irrelevant to the concerns that real writers have in the real world. Quite the contrary: They go to the flabby heart of a terminally opaque style.

But however prescriptive I seem about what counts as clear writing, don't you be reluctant to experiment, to play with different prose styles. Try writing in the ponderous bureaucratic style that this book condemns, simply to get the feel of writing it. Try creating a passage in a style elegant beyond your needs, just to see whether you can pull it off. Try writing the longest sentence you can, just to feel when you've stretched it to its breaking point. Try writing a passage of one curt sentence after another to achieve a sense of breathless haste, or of utter certitude.

Language, style, should not be something that boxes you in,

but a means to free your intellect and imagination from the obscurity that confused prose puts between you and your ideas.

To Teachers

This book addresses only one aspect of composition: style. It does not take up matters of intention, invention, or organization. Their omission is not an oversight. I intend this to be a short book focusing on the single most serious problem that *mature* writers face: a wordy, tangled, too-complex prose style. For larger matters of form, you will need another book.

I have tried to approach style as process, as an achievement. The first step in that process, of course, is to get something down on paper. But that's the easy part. The serious part of writing is rewriting. Samuel Johnson said it about as well as anyone: "What is written without effort is in general read without pleasure." The effort is more in the editing than in the writing.

I know that many undergraduates have a problem precisely opposite to that which most of this book addresses—a style characterized by one fifteen-word sentence after another. But that's not a problem that seems to endure very long. I have worked with a good many adult writers in government, in the professions, and in business; I have met not one whose major writing problem was a style that was immature. I am encouraged in this observation by every other adult writing program I have ever seen: Not one of them takes up the matter of writing longer rather than shorter sentences.

Now, you might object that there is still no point in addressing a problem that does not yet afflict your students. Two points: First, dealing with this matter now will prepare them to deal with a problem that many seem destined to develop later. To assume that we should not address a problem before it arises is a little bit like teaching birth control after the rabbit dies.

And second, simply by writing out the new sentences that result from editing those in the exercises, students will come to feel what it is like to write down a sentence longer than ten or fifteen words. Copy and imitation, time-honored ways of teaching writing, will help the less advanced students feel the rhythm and movement that a long but clear sentence demands. After all, if we cannot lead our students through what they are supposed to be learning to do, we ought not be surprised when they do not learn to do it.

The exercises in imitation are directed specifically toward developing a mature style. Assure your students that they don't have to imitate the model sentences word for word; they have only to imitate the stylistic point being discussed. If they have problems thinking up things to write about, suggest some topics parallel to the subject matter of the model sentences. In fact, you might do the exercises yourself to get a sense of what can and can't be done with them.

All this is intended to anticipate an objection that some readers may raise: The material is appropriate for upper-class students and adults but too difficult for beginning students. I understand why some teachers of freshmen might feel that way. I realize how severely underprepared many first-year students are in matters of both style and grammar. I use a few grammatical terms here. But I confess I am a bit puzzled that any teacher would object to a discussion that introduces terms that a student does not know but should. I have always assumed that we are in the business of teaching students what they do not know, and that if they do not know what *subject, verb, predicate, object,* and so on mean, then we tell them. I don't see how we can avoid using some terminology, even new terminology, any more than a physicist can avoid using new terms such as *lepton, quark,* or *charmed particle* in a textbook on the fundamental structure of matter.

Lesson Nine on style and usage may disconcert more than a few. (Indeed, it already has.) It asserts that some widely circulated "rules" of usage may in fact not be as widely observed by genuinely careful writers as some might think, or wish. Parts of that lesson may read as if I based my observations on some quirky notions of personal usage, privately arrived at. In fact, I have based them on a good deal of reading, done specifically to find whether those "rules" have any force among otherwise careful writers. I can only assert that in writing which has not been thoroughly edited to make it conform to the "rules" I address, there appear a good many singular *data*s, a good many *which*es for *that*s, a good many prepositions at the ends of sentences, split infinitives, sentences beginning with *and*. Indeed, all these so-called violations of good usage appear in books that have been scrupulously edited.

In the real world of real writers, success depends little on avoiding *contact* as verb or *finalize* meaning more than finish. It depends on the ability to make a point precisely, directly, and persuasively.

"Precision" and "Upholding Standards" have too often meant finding trivial points of usage violated in prose that deserves criticism on far more substantial grounds. Coming down hard on a *which* that we think should be a *that* has for too long been a way of saying, "I don't like what I'm reading very much, but I don't know how else to express my dislike." It is the equivalent of that all-purpose "Awk" that so many among us scribble in the margin when they can't explain what *makes* a sentence awkward.

I hope that what follows will provide a vocabulary that makes the word *precision* more than an expression of imprecise values, and *imprecise* more often an expression of precise displeasure.

To All

Devoured in one piece, this book will surely seem indigestible. It does not have the leisurely pace of an occasional essay that can be read in one or two sittings. The lessons are compact: Read quickly, they will seem dense, even overwhelming. Take them in small chunks. Do a section at a time, up to the exercises. Do the exercises; find someone else's writing to edit; edit some old writing of your own. Then look hard at what you've written today—first only for the point of the lesson, or section. Then go through it a second time, looking for another point, and if you have the time, again for other points. If you try to edit everything at once, a sentence will dissolve into a confusion of words.

So many have provided useful criticism and welcome support that I cannot possibly thank them all. But I must begin with my English 194 students, who put up with so many badly typed and faintly dittoed pages and with a teacher who was at times as puzzled over matters of style as they. Their interest in clear and concise writing compensated for a lot of tedious hours spent editing their papers. They were a pleasure to teach, and their subsequent comments about the importance of what they have learned have been gratifying. I thank them all.

I have considerable intellectual debts to those who have broken ground in psycholinguistics, text linguistics, discourse analysis, functional sentence perspective, and so on. Those of you who keep up with such matters will recognize the influence of Charles Fillmore, Jan Firbas, Nils Enkvist, Michael Halliday, Noam Chomsky, Thomas Bever, Vic Yngve, and others. I know I have been influenced more than a little by Robert Graves and Alan Hodge, H. B. Fowler, H. L. Mencken, and surely by E. B. White. I would like to think that I have made explicit what Mr. White advises writers to do and what he himself has done for so long. Maine air must be, I think, a powerful astringent to style.

I am very grateful to colleagues who have taken time from their own busy lives to read the work of another. At such times, the word *community* in Community of Scholars takes on a special meaning. Whatever quality this book may have is due in large part to their care, time, and energy. I must thank in particular Randy Berlin, Ken Bruffee, Douglas Butturff, Donald Byker, Bruce Campbell, Elaine Chaika, Avon Crismore, Don Freeman, Constance Gefvert, Maxine Hairston, George Hoffman, Ted Lowe, Susan Miller, Neil Nakadate, Mike Pownall, Peter Priest, Margaret Shaklee, Nancy Sommers, Mary Taylor, and Stephen Witte.

I would also like to acknowledge the assistance of Frederick C. Mish, editorial director, G. & C. Merriam Company, in locating the best examples of three citations in Lesson Nine.

The editors at Scott, Foresman saved me from more than a few stylistic gaffes, especially Dave Ebbitt, whose editing pen has a very sharp point.

I would like to thank most profoundly the editor who first urged me to write this book, Harriett Prentiss. I am most grateful to her.

And finally, to my family—my thanks for your love and support and understanding, especially when Daddy's "just one minute" stretched to an hour or two.

Joseph M. Williams

Preface to Second Edition

The generous reception accorded the first edition of *Style* was, needless to say, gratifying. It would have been easy to make a few minor adjustments in the text and layout and send it out again. But at the risk of fixing what may not have been broken, I have made some major changes in the book. I hope that I have removed nothing of consequence, and that everything I have added makes sense. I have rewritten the Lesson on topics and stress as two Lessons and reshuffled the overall order, putting topic and stress directly after the Lesson on agents and actions. The agent/action principles now lead directly into issues of topic and stress. Together, they provide the most powerful insight one can offer into the complexities of style. The topic/stress Lesson can now also inform the discussion about long sentences.

This new order also makes it possible to divide the book into three parts. The first part consists of basic Lessons on agents and actions, topics and stresses, and simple wordiness. The second part consists of Lessons on managing long sentences and on more complex issues of elegance. The third part consists of Lessons on usage and punctuation.

I have also cleaned up the exercises. I had originally hoped that they would be progressively more difficult, rehearsing problems of earlier Lessons while simultaneously providing material for the current Lesson. That led to unnecessary confusion. More of the exercises now address strictly the issue of the Lesson in which they appear.

Scott, Foresman's designers have substantially changed the layout and typography. I trust that the format and design now more clearly reflect the structure of the Lessons.

Again, I would like to thank those colleagues who helped improve this second edition: Anne Burley, Patricia Davis, Alger N. Doane, George Gopen, Michael Orth, Linda Shamoon, Harry E. Shaw, and Steven D. Stark. Two colleagues have substantially helped me clarify many issues of style. Our collaboration in creating the advanced writing program in the College at the University of Chicago has contributed immeasurably to bringing into focus more issues than are contained in this small book. They are Greg Colomb and Frank Kinahan. I would also like to thank Don Freeman for catching a careless allusion in Lesson Eight.

I must acknowledge and thank two whose advice has contributed mightily to whatever has improved this second edition. Constance Rajala has patiently but firmly insisted on my doing whatever had to be done when it had to be done. And Dave Ebbitt has again given me a lesson in editing. I have never had a better editor.

And once again my gratitude and love to those who have helped make it a pleasure to write at all—Joe, Megan, Chris, and Joan.

J. M. W.

CONTENTS

Toward Clarity

If thought corrupts language, language can also corrupt thought.

GEORGE ORWELL

Everything that can be thought at all can be thought clearly. Everything that can be said can be said clearly.

LUDWIG WITTGENSTEIN

Have something to say, and say it as clearly as you can. That is the only secret of style.

MATTHEW ARNOLD

To me, style is just the outside of content, and content the inside of style, like the outside and inside of the human body—both go together, they can't be separated.

JEAN-LUC GODARD

With precious few exceptions, all the books on style in English are by writers quite unable to write.

H. L. MENCKEN

T his is a short book with a simple thesis: it's good to write clearly, and anyone can.

No one would argue with the first part of that claim, least of all those who regularly have to translate prose like this:

> There is now no effective mechanism for introducing
> into the initiation and development stages of reporting
> requirements information on existing reporting and
> guidance on how to minimize burden associations with
> new requirements.

But that second part might be disputed by a good many who labor at writing clearly but still end up with prose that hides their ideas not just from their readers but sometimes even from themselves.

Now, we can write prose that fails for reasons more important than an obscure style. If we're as confused about a point when we finish a job of writing as when we began, our writing will be confused too. If we ignore what our readers have to know if they're to understand our ideas, then what we write will surely bewilder them. And if we can't find a way to organize our ideas clearly for our specific audience, then what we write will almost certainly lack that sense of direction and purpose that all coherent prose demands.

But important as those problems are, this book specifically addresses a different matter: Once we've learned how to write sentences that are grammatically correct and acceptably punctuated, once we've learned how to focus our ideas, how to gather and organize the information we need to move a clearly defined audience to a specific end, we still have to get those ideas down on paper in a form that is not just grammatically correct, but clear and concise enough to be effective.

That is the aim of this book: to explain how you can overcome the one problem that has afflicted generations of mature writers—the problem of an unnecessarily complex prose style. When we find this kind of writing in government regulations and directives, we call it *bureaucratese;* when we find it in contracts and judicial pronouncements, we call it *legalese;* when we find it in scholarly articles and books that inflate simple ideas into gassy abstractions, we call it *academese.* Partly because we find it almost everywhere we look, some believe that it must be the style of institutional success. It is more often the style of academic pretension or bureaucratic intimidation. Whenever we find it, it is a style that, once we see through it, must finally infuriate us.

But anyone familiar with English prose has to wonder whether we can do anything that will substantially improve it. In the early sixteenth century, when English first became respectable enough to replace French and Latin as England's institutional language, our first impulse toward elegance produced a prose style thick with Latinate abstraction, a weakness to which many English writers have surrendered ever since.

By the middle of the seventeenth century, an inflated style had infected the sciences. Shortly after the Royal Society was established in 1660, one of its historians complained.

> . . . of all the studies of men, nothing may sooner be obtained than this vicious abundance of phrase, this trick of metaphors, this volubility of tongue which makes so great a noise in the world. . . .
> —Thomas Sprat, *History of the Royal Society,* 1667

When the New World was settled, we had a chance to create a lean and sinewy prose style to suit a people civilizing a continent. But American writers no more escaped chronic bloat and abstraction than did the English. James Fenimore Cooper asserted, not too simply and directly himself, that "the common faults of American language are an ambition of effect, a want of simplicity, and a turgid abuse of terms." Henry David Thoreau agreed: "All men are really attracted by the beauty of plain speech [but they] write in a florid style in imitation of this."

We read the same sentiments today. On the language of the social sciences:

> . . . a turgid and polysyllabic prose does seem to prevail in the social sciences. . . . Such a lack of ready intelligibility, I believe, usually has little or nothing to do with the complexity of thought. It has to do almost entirely with certain confusions of the academic writer about his own status.
> —C. Wright Mills, *The Sociological Imagination*

On the language of medicine:

> It now appears that obligatory obfuscation is a firm tradition
> within the medical profession. . . . [Medical writing] is a
> highly skilled, calculated attempt to confuse the
> reader. . . . A doctor feels he might get passed over for an
> assistant professorship because he wrote his papers too
> clearly—because he made his ideas seem too simple.
>
> —Michael Crichton, *New England Journal of Medicine*

And on the language of law:

> . . . in law journals, in speeches, in classrooms and in
> courtrooms, lawyers and judges are beginning to worry
> about how often they have been misunderstood, and they
> are discovering that sometimes they cannot even understand
> each other.
>
> —Tom Goldstein, *New York Times*

(The abuse heaped on the prose of government bureaucrats is too
familiar to need special testimony here.)

Most adults, I suspect, write in these ways for some combination of just two or three reasons. Michael Crichton cited the first: We use complicated language to hide not only simple ideas but even their absence. Impenetrable prose will impress those who confuse difficulty with substance—and there are many who do. Why else so much turgid writing?

In the same way, we use difficult and therefore intimidating language to protect what we have from those who want a share of it: the power, prestige, and privilege that go with being part of the ruling class. We can keep knowledge from those who would use it by locking it up, but we can also hide ideas behind language so impenetrable that only those trained to translate it can find them.

Another reason some of us write badly is that we are seized by the memory of an English teacher for whom the only kind of good writing was writing free from errors which only that teacher could understand: fused genitives, dangling participles, split infinitives, and other exotic *disjecta membra*. For many such writers, a blank page is now a minefield they traverse gingerly, preoccupied less with clarity and precision than with sheer survival.

But the most common reason for bad writing is, I think, the simplest: Most writers have just never learned how to write clearly and directly in the first place. No one has ever told them how to edit syntactic confusion into clear prose. Or even that they should try. I say this because I have never met anyone who was anything but delighted to learn the few simple rules needed to edit an unreadable tangle into clear, straightforward prose.

Now, in fact, when we address the matter of clear prose, we indirectly address some of those more general problems that I referred to before—problems of organization, intention, and audience. The very act of writing and rewriting helps us to clarify our ideas, to understand better what we want to say, to find the best way to organize our material, to speak to the real interests and needs of our readers. If we can't see through our own confused style to the substance of our ideas, we won't be able to understand ourselves well enough to use the act of writing to sharpen our ideas, our organization, and our intentions. When we write page after page of impenetrable prose, we finally lose track of our train of thought: The mere effort to find our way through every sentence finally distracts us from the substance of our ideas.

Writing can be a fruitfully circular process: We have to understand what we want to say in order to write it clearly and concisely. But if we can't write what we mean clearly and concisely enough or, when necessary, clearly though complexly enough, we won't be able to understand exactly what we are—or could be—saying. If we can write and then quickly rewrite syntactic confusion into clear prose, we'll understand our ideas better. And when we understand our ideas better, we'll write more clearly, and if we write more clearly, we'll understand even better . . . and so it goes, until we run out of energy, interest, or time.

For some of us, that moment may come months or years after we begin. But for most of us, it's close to tomorrow morning. Few of us enjoy the luxury of ruminating for weeks and months over our prose, writing and rewriting to sculpt our ideas in a leisurely and reflective sort of way, polishing every phrase and clause to a lapidary finish. Most of us have to be satisfied with a less polished but still useful product.

That limitation only makes a clear, direct style more important: If we don't have the time to ponder over every sentence as we write, we have to be able to get our ideas down quickly and surely the first time, and then to edit our first draft into something clear, simple, and direct.

But as important as directness and clarity may be, there are times when we want to go beyond it, to a style that is a bit more self-consciously crafted, to a style that may even be just a bit elegant.

> Now the trumpet summons us again—not as a call to bear arms, though arms we need; not as a call to battle, though embattled we are; but a call to bear the burden of a long twilight struggle, year in and year out, "rejoicing in hope, patient in tribulation," a struggle against the common enemies of man: tyranny, poverty, disease and war itself.
> —John F. Kennedy, Inaugural Address, January 20, 1961

Not all of us are called upon to write a Presidential Inaugural Address, but sometimes our intentions, our sense of who we are, require that we invest even our most modest prose with more than simple clarity. The last few lessons speak to that matter.

About fifty years ago, H. L. Mencken wrote,

> With precious few exceptions, all the books on style in English are by writers quite unable to write. The subject, indeed, seems to exercise a special and dreadful fascination over school ma'ams, bucolic college professors, and other such pseudoliterates. . . . Their central aim, of course, is to reduce the whole thing to a series of simple rules—the overmastering passion of their melancholy order, at all times and everywhere.

This melancholy judgment has hovered over every sentence I've written here. And Mencken is right: No one can teach a clear style by rule, simple or not, especially to those who have nothing to say and no reason to say it, to those who cannot think or feel or see.

But I know that many do think carefully and feel deeply and see clearly but still cannot write well. I also know that learning to write well can help us think and feel and see and that in fact there are some simple and straightforward principles that help.

Here they are.

The Grammar of Clarity

Suit the action to the word, the word to the action.

WILLIAM SHAKESPEARE, *HAMLET,* 3.2

Action is eloquence.

WILLIAM SHAKESPEARE, *CORIOLANUS,* 3.2

We don't lack words to praise good writing: clear, direct, readable, precise. But words like these reflect only how we *feel* about writing: they don't tell us what good writing *is*. We need a way to talk about writing that tells us what is there on the page that makes us feel as we do. Some measures of good writing, for example, simply ask us to count the number of syllables and words and clauses* (the fewer the better, according to most).[1]

But if for every sentence* we wrote, we had to count every syllable and word and clause, we'd spend more time counting than writing. And even if counting did tell us which sentences were more or less easy to read, we wouldn't need to count if we learned in the first place simply to sense when a passage was clear and direct, or tangled and obscure.

We don't have to count syllables and words in these two sentences to recognize which is clear and which isn't:

> Our lack of pertinent data prevented determination of committee action effectiveness in fund targeting to areas of greatest assistance need.

> Because we lacked pertinent data, we could not determine whether the committee had targeted funds to areas that needed assistance the most.

The real difference between those two sentences isn't in the number of words or syllables or clauses, but in how the writer organizes what he wants to say, how he uses subjects* and verbs* to express who is—or is not—doing what to whom. If we are going to understand why that second sentence is more precise, more direct, we have to understand how the nouns* and verbs, subjects and objects* of those two sentences support the ideas they express.

A FIRST PRINCIPLE

We can state the first principle of clear writing easily enough:

> State who's doing what in the subject of your sentence, and state what that "who" is doing in your verb.

[1]Throughout this book, terms marked with an asterisk* are defined in the Appendix.

In the second example sentence above, the writer names who acts in the subject of each clause or who is responsible for each action*, and tells in specific verbs what those actors do:

Subject/Agent		Verb/Action
we	⟶	lacked
we	⟶	could not determine
the committee	⟶	targeted
areas	⟶	needed

In the first sentence, on the other hand, the writer hides who is doing what to whom. He expresses actions not in verbs but in abstract nouns: *lack, determination, action, assistance, need.* And the writer identifies the agents, the doers of those actions not in subjects, but in prepositional phrases* or in modifiers tacked onto nouns:

Our lack . . . committee action effectiveness . . . areas

Or the agent of the action doesn't appear in the sentence at all. For example, how do we know who determines effectiveness?

Our lack of pertinent data prevented (whose?) determination . . .

In the clearer, more direct sentence, the writer used subjects, verbs, and objects—the major sentence parts—to state his meaning directly. In the first sentence, the writer did not.

There are other principles of good writing, and in the following lessons we'll get to them. But this first principle—express actions in verbs, and identify the agents of those actions in subjects—goes to the heart of a clear style. Get that straight, and the rest of the sentence falls into place.

VERBS AND ACTIONS

A clear and direct style depends most importantly on how we express action. As we'll use the word here, action will cover many notions: movement, feeling, process, change, activity, condition—physical or mental, literal or figurative. The important point is this: Although we cannot always express crucial actions in verbs, in the clearest and most vigorous sentences we usually do. Compare the verbs in these pairs of sentences.

> There **will be** a suspension of these programs by the dean until his reevaluation of their progress **has occurred.**
> The dean **will suspend** these programs until he **reevaluates** their progress.

> At the time of several congressional committee investigations of the CIA, they **performed** no intelligence collection analysis.
> Several congressional committees **investigated** the CIA, but they **did not analyze** how the CIA **collected** intelligence data.

Suspend and *reevaluate* are more specific than *be* and *occur. Investigated, collected,* and *analyzed* are more specific than *performed.*

 In the next four sentences, the meaning becomes increasingly clear as the actions become increasingly specific:

> There **has been** the exercise of effective staff information dissemination control on the part of the secretary.
> The secretary **has exercised** effective staff information dissemination control.
> The secretary **has** effectively **controlled** staff information dissemination.
> The secretary **has** effectively **controlled** the way the staff **disseminates** information.

The crucial actions aren't *be* or *exercise* but *control* and *disseminate.*

 When we regularly express crucial actions not as verbs, but as nouns, our prose will become like that confused and sluggish writing so common in government, business, and the professions. In chronically indirect and tangled prose, the writer expresses the action of paying not by the verb *pay* but by the noun *payment* (or the pretentious *compensation);* the act of studying not by the verb *study,* but by the noun *study* (or the more weighty and wordy *in-depth investigation);* the action of needing not by the verbs *need* or *must* but by the noun *need* (or the more turgid *urgent requirement).* And then the writer clumps those nouns together into a long compound* noun phrase. As a consequence, we have to wade through,

> There is a student loan repayment reliability study need.

or worse,

> There is an urgent requirement for a student loan recompensation reliability in-depth investigation.

instead of skimming through,

> We must find out how reliably students repay their loans.

Most writers of turgid prose use their verbs not to express specific actions but merely to state that those actions exist:

We **conducted** an *investigation* of it.	=	We **investigated** it.
A *need* **exists** for greater candidate *selection efficiency*.	=	We **must select** candidates more **efficiently.**
There **is** the *possibility* of prior *approval* of it.	=	He **may approve** of it ahead of time.
A *review* **was done** of the relevant regulations.	=	They **reviewed** the relevant regulations.
We **had** a *discussion* of the matter.	=	We **discussed** the matter.
The establishment of a different *approach* on the part of the committee **has become** a *necessity*.	=	The committee **has to approach** it differently.

When your prose seems out of focus, fuzzy and imprecise, look for the important action, the central process or condition. If it typically appears in a noun, set off between empty verbs and prepositions, your style surely suffers from that bloat and abstraction that makes so much institutional prose thoroughly unreadable. Recast the sentence. Put the crucial action in the verb. And if an important condition or quality is expressed in a noun instead of an adjective* or adverb*, get rid of the noun and use the adjective or adverb:

> There was *precision* in the *preparation* of the data.
> They *prepared* the data *precisely*.

> She exhibited considerable *intelligence* in regard to that.
> She was *intelligent* about that.

We call a noun derived from a verb or adjective a nominalization*,

a word that is itself a noun made out of a verb, nominalize. Here
are some examples:

Verb	> Nominalization	Adjective	> Nominalization
discover	discovery	careless	carelessness
move	movement	difficult	difficulty
resist	resistance	different	difference
react	reaction	elegant	elegance
hope	hope	equal	equality

Nominalization sounds like jargon, but it's a useful term. It expresses in a single word what most afflicts a sentence such as,

> There is a *need* for *reanalysis* of our data.

or worse,

> There is a data *reanalysis need.*

instead of,

> We *must reanalyze* our data.

SUBJECTS AND AGENTS

Just as a verb and an action seem naturally to go together, so do
subject and agent*. An agent is the source, the party or thing
ultimately responsible for the action or condition that a sentence
refers to. And we can immediately recognize what happens to a
style when that agent appears some place other than the subject
(usually because we've nominalized our important verbs):

> Determination of foreign policy takes place at the *presidential*
> level.
> *The President* determines foreign policy.

> A need for a reevaluation of his condition by *a doctor* exists.
> A *doctor* should reevaluate his condition.

Notice that in both cases, the second sentence is more direct, more
personal, because the agent appears in the subject and the impor-

tant action appears in the verb. In many cases, we don't just dislocate the agent; we drop it out altogether—most often in a passive* sentence. Compare the passive (which here omits the agent) and the more explicit active* (which states the agent in the subject):

> Passive: Who should be admitted to nuclear energy facilities has not yet been determined.

> Active: *The Nuclear Regulatory Commission* has not yet determined whom it should admit to nuclear energy facilities.

Nominalizations also let us drop out the agent:

> A *need* for a *reevaluation* of his condition exists. (who needs? who reevaluates?)
> The *discovery* in regard to the *identification* and *classification* of mutant genes has been acknowledged. (who discovers? identifies? classifies? acknowledges?)
> There is as yet an *absence* of nuclear energy facility access *determination*. (who determines?)

There are different kinds of agents, including collective agents:

> *Faculties* that achieve national eminence do not always do the best teaching.

secondary or remote agents:

> *Mayor Daley* built Chicago into a giant among cities.

and even figurative agents that stand for the real agents:

> *The White House* announced today the end of price controls.
> *The business sector* refuses to cooperate in the establishment of guidelines.
> *Most instances of malignant tumors* fail to seek prompt medical attention.

In some sentences, we use subjects to name things that are really the means, the instrument, by which some unstated agent performs its action.

> *Studies* of coal production reveal these figures.
> *These new data* establish the need for more detailed analysis.
> *This evidence* proves my theory.

That is,

> When *we study* coal production, we find these figures.
> *I have established* through these new data that we must analyze the problem in more detail.
> With this evidence *I can prove* my theory.

Regardless of the precise sense of agency we express in a subject, whether it's literal or figurative, a real agency or its instrument, the first principle of a clear and direct style remains the same:

> As often as you can, use verbs to express the central action and use the subject of that verb to express a strong sense of its agency.

Now we have to understand that this principle is only a useful guide, not an exceptionless rule. Later you will look at sentences where, to be clear, you have to violate it. But if you *consistently* express action in abstract nouns and *consistently* use verbs such as *do, make, have, be, perform, occur*—verbs that are almost meaningless because they are so general—then you are probably writing prose that is both graceless and unclear. There is no golden mean to aim at, no ideal proportion of nominalizations (though more than one in every six or seven words will almost always prove to be too many). The point is to develop a sense of when your prose moves with the clarity and vigor that only precise subjects and strong verbs provide. And to know how to revise your prose when it doesn't.

OBJECTS AND GOALS

As agent is to subject and action is to verb, so goal* is to object:

subject	verb	object
agent	action	goal

A goal is that toward which an agent directs its action or attention. It's whatever is changed, affected, created, attended to, influenced, transformed, moved, as a result of some other force.

One of the traditional definitions of a direct object* is a noun that "receives" the action of a transitive* verb:

We described *the scene.*
Japan has exported *large amounts of steel.*
Local politics reflect *grass roots sentiments.*

We ordinarily express a goal as a direct object:

Shakespeare wrote *Hamlet.*

But there are exceptions. A goal appears in the subject of a passive verb:

Hamlet was written by Shakespeare.

The goal can also be the subject of a small number of active* verbs:

His ideas received my constant criticism.
The personnel experienced a sharp cutback.
Our recommendations went through several reviews.

It's useful to be able to identify objects and goals, but the more important parts of a sentence are its subject and agent, its verb and action. When subjects and verbs clearly express agents and their actions, the objects and goals will usually take care of themselves. Get the sentence off to a good start and the rest of the sentence will take care of itself.

LOOKING FOR NOMINALIZATIONS

A few common patterns of abstract nominalizations are easy to spot and revise.

1. When the nominalization is the subject of an empty verb, change the nominalization to a verb and find a new subject:

Our *intention* **is** to audit the records of the program.
We *intend* to audit the records of the program.

Our *discussion* **concerned** a tax cut.
We *discussed* a tax cut.

2. When the nominalization follows an empty verb, change the nominalization to a verb that can replace the empty verb.

> The police **conducted** an *investigation* into the matter.
> The police *investigated* the matter.
> The committee **has** no *expectation* that it will meet the deadline.
> The committee does not *expect* to meet the deadline.

3. When the nominalization follows a *there is* or *there are,* change the nominalization to a verb that replaces the *is* or *are* and find a subject:

> There is a *need* for further *study* of this program.
> The engineering staff *must study* this program further.
>
> There was considerable *erosion* of the land from the floods.
> The floods considerably *eroded* the land.

4. When a nominalization in a subject is linked to another nominalization in the predicate* by a verb or a phrase that expresses some kind of logical connection such as cause and effect, condition and consequence, revise as follows:
    (a) Change both abstractions to verbs,
    (b) find the subject of those verbs, and,
    (c) link the new clauses with a word that expresses the logical connection.

> To express cause: *because, since, when*
> To express condition: *if, provided that*
> To express reservation: *though, although*

Schematically, we do this:

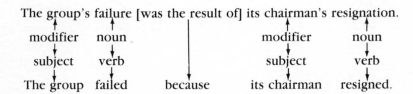

Data *analysis* must be done immediately after its *collection.*

The data must be *analyzed* immediately *after* it is *collected*.

And we could make this active, with agents in the subject position:

You must analyze the data immediately after *you collect* it.

Some further examples:

The *discovery* of a method for the *manufacture* of artificial skin
will have the result of a great increase in the *survival* of patients
with radical burns.
—Researchers *discover* a way to *manufacture* artificial skin. . . .
—More patients *will survive* radical burns. . . .
If researchers can discover a way to manufacture artificial skin,
many more patients will survive radical burns.

The presence of extensive rust *damage* to the exterior surfaces
prevented immediate *repairs* to the hull.
—Rust had extensively *damaged* the exterior surfaces. . . .
—We could not *repair* the hull immediately. . . .
Because rust had extensively damaged the exterior surfaces, we
could not repair the hull immediately.

The *instability* of the motor housing did not preclude the *completion* of the field trials.
—The motor housing was *unstable*. . . .
—The research staff *completed* field trials. . . .
Even though the motor housing was unstable, the research staff
completed the field trials.

5. When you have two nominalizations in a row, turn at least the
    first into a verb. Then either leave the second as it is or turn it
    into a verb in a clause beginning with *how* or *why:*

There was first a *review* of the *evolution* of the medial dorsal fin.
First, she *reviewed* the *evolution* of the medial dorsal fin.
First, she *reviewed how* the medial dorsal fin *evolved*.

The President could offer no *explanation* for his *popularity
decline*.
The President could not *explain* his *popularity decline*.
The President could not *explain* why his popularity had *declined*.

USEFUL NOMINALIZATIONS

In some cases, nominalizations are useful, even necessary. Don't try to get rid of these.

1. The nominalization is a subject referring to a previous sentence:

    These arguments all depend on a single unproven claim.
    This decision can lead to costly consequences.
    Such an agreement is in everyone's best interests.

Nominalizations like these let us link sentences into a more cohesive flow.

2 . The nominalization names what would be the object of its verb:

    I do not understand either *her meaning* or *his intention.*

rather than the wordier:

    I do not understand either *what she means* or *what he intends.*

We don't improve these much by changing nominalizations into clauses.

3. *The fact that* will usually yield to a more succinct nominalization:

    The fact that I denied what he accused me of impressed the jury.
    My denial of his accusations impressed the jury.

4. Some nominalizations are so well established that they serve as useful shorthand.

    Few issues have so deeply divided American politics as *abortion* on *demand.*
    The Equal Rights *Amendment* was an issue in past *elections.*
    Taxation without *representation* was not the central concern of the American *Revolution.*

In each of those sentences, the abstract nominalization refers to an idea that we refer to over and over again. Rather than spell out that idea every time in a full-blown clause, we contract it into a single noun that is more concise than the full clause. And, of course, some nominalizations name abstract ideas that we can express only in nominalizations: *freedom, death, love, hope, life, wisdom.* If we couldn't turn some verbs or adjectives into nouns, we would find it difficult—perhaps impossible—to discuss those subjects that have preoccupied us for millennia. You simply have to develop an eye for the nominalization that expresses one of these ideas and the nominalization that hides a significant action:

> There has been a *demand* for an end to *taxation* on entertainment.
> We *demand* that the government not *tax* entertainment.

Exercise 1–1

Rewrite these sentences in a more direct style. In 1–5, both agents and actions are in italics. State the agents as subjects and the actions or conditions as verbs or adjectives.

1. *Our expectation* was to establish new tolerance levels.
2. *Attempts* were made on the part of the *engineering staff* in regard to an *assessment* of the project.
3. There were *expectations* by the *governing committee* that *their* report *submission* would meet the deadline.
4. The *appearance* of the *candidate* before the board was on June 30.
5. *The governor's refusal* of the request is a *necessity.*

In 6–10, only agents are in italics.

6. A *presidential* appeal was made to *the American people* for the conservation of gasoline.
7. More accurate measurements of the thorium half-life were conducted at that time by *independent investigators.*
8. Discussions by the *participants* of the future of the program were conducted amicably.
9. There was no independent *business-sector* analysis of the cause of the trade deficit.

10.   Agreement as to the need for revisions in the terms of the treaty was reached by *the two sides.*

In 11–15, only the nominalizations are in italics.

11.   There was *uneasiness* among management over the result of the survey.
12.   There must be thorough *preparation* of the specimen sections by the laboratory personnel.
13.   The discrepancy in the data demands *checking* by the insurer.
14.   The *rejection* of the application by the dean was unexpected.
15.   The performance by the police of an *investigation* into the affair occured without delay.

In the next ten items, neither agent nor action is identified. Where no agent is expressed, invent one.

16.   There should be no hesitation in regard to saying no.
17.   The same principles of bilateral symmetry received study after the last report.
18.   A solution to the problem of UFOs will never be found by the Air Force.
19.   It is my belief that there should be consultation by the administrators with the student body before changes in rules are made.
20.   Cutbacks in loan availability are mandated as a result of lack of success in the acquisition of federal funding.
21.   A redetermination of their personnel needs is necessary before assistance from local sources can be provided.
22.   Complete replacement of corneal tissue depends on the successful suppression of immunoresponse mechanisms.
23.   It would be an oversimplification of the problem for me to put forth the argument that all government officials engage in inefficient and wasteful administrative behavior.
24.   A significant contribution to the literature on the subject is Goywzc's specification of the causes for emigration from environments with a lack of sufficient capital base.
25.   While methods for the corroboration of reliability and validity of respondents' responses have been under development by social scientists, there were none employed in the present study, making reliance on respondents' exaggerated estimates of their situation fraught with unreliability.

PASSIVES

In addition to avoiding abstract nominalizations, you can make your style more vigorous and direct if you also avoid *unnecessary* passive verbs. Now there are many occasions when you should *choose* the passive; we'll look at some of those occasions in a moment. But when you use passives in sentence after sentence, your style will slow to a crawl. And when you combine passives with nominalizations, you will have created that wretched prose we call medicalese, sociologese, educationese, bureaucratese—all of the *-eses* of those who confuse authority and objectivity with polysyllabic abstraction and remote impersonality.

In passive sentences, the subject expresses the goal of an action; a form of *be* always precedes a past participle* form of the verb; and the agent may or may not be expressed in a *by*-phrase:

Active: The partners   broke   the agreement.

Passive: The agreement   was broken   (by the partners).

The passive order reverses the more direct order of agent-action-goal; it will eventually cripple the easy movement of an otherwise energetic style.

Compare these passages:

It *was found* that information concerning energy resources allocated to the states *was not obtained*. This action *is need-ed* so that a determination of redirection *is permitted* on a timely basis when weather conditions change. A system *must be established* so that information on weather condi-tions and fuel consumption *may be gathered* on a regular basis.

We *found* that the Department of Energy *did not obtain* in-formation about energy resources that federal offices were allocating to the states. The department *needs* this informa-tion so that it *can determine* how to *redirect* these resources when weather conditions change. The secretary of the department *must establish* a system so that his office *can gather* information on weather conditions and fuel con-sumption on a regular basis.

The second passage is not only more fluent but also more specific and informative. We know who is supposed to be doing what.

To choose between the active and the passive, ask two questions: First, must your audience know who is performing the action? Second, are you able to maintain a logical consistency in the subjects of your sentences?

Often, we deliberately avoid stating who is responsible for an action, because we don't know or don't care or because we'd rather not say:

> Between July 2 and July 9, over 5,000 brochures *were printed.*
> If a person *is found* guilty, he *can be sued* for losses.
> The records *were kept* in a safe.

In sentences like these, the passive is the natural and correct choice.

> Because the final safety inspection *was* neither *performed* nor *monitored,* the brake plate assembly mechanism *was left* incorrectly aligned, information that *was known* several months before it *was* publicly *revealed.*

More often, though, writers use the passive out of habit and so they simply neglect to assign responsibility. In the example about energy, for instance, the writer of the original passage probably took it for granted that his audience knew who was supposed to be obtaining information, setting up systems, and so on.

The second question is whether the subjects of your sentences are consistent. If in a series of passive sentences, you find yourself constantly shifting from one subject to another, try rewriting those sentences in the active.

Use the beginning of a sentence to orient a reader to what follows. If in a series of sentences we give our reader no consistent starting point, then that stretch of writing will seem less coherent than it might be. Look again at the subjects in the pair of paragraphs about energy. In the first version, the subjects of the passive sentences seem to be chosen almost at random.

> It . . . information. . . . This action . . . a
> determination. . . . A system . . . information. . . .

In the second, the active sentences provide the reader with a con-

sistent point of view; the writer "stages" the sentences from a consistent string of subjects:

> We . . . Department of Energy . . . federal offices. . . . The
> department . . . it. . . . The secretary of the department . . .
> his office. . . .

Each subject anchors the reader in something familiar before he
moves on to something new.

On the other hand, when the goal can be made a consistent
subject, then the passive is appropriate:

> By the first six months of 1945, it was clear to the world
> that *the Axis nations* had been essentially defeated, that all
> that remained was the final, but bloody, climax. The *borders
> of Germany* had been breached, and *both Germany and
> Japan* were being bombed around the clock. *Neither coun-
> try,* though, had been so devastated that it could not resist.

We will return to this question in Lesson Two.

The Institutional Passive

Passives in official and academic prose raise a special problem
because prejudice against the first-person *I* or *we* is so widespread.
Many writers of scholarly prose, and large numbers of teachers,
believe—mistakenly—that editors will not accept

> After *we irrigated* the peritoneal cavity with saline solution, *we in-
> troduced* an acrylic-fiber viewer.

but demand

> After the peritoneal cavity *was irrigated* with saline solution, an
> acrylic-fiber viewer *was introduced.*

Scientific writing in particular, they believe, demands an aloof,
third-person style to demonstrate the author's objectivity—or at
least modesty. Yet we have only to glance at some of the best
scientific journals to discover instance after instance of *we* as a subject. Here are the first few words from several consecutive
sentences in an article in *Science,* a highly prestigious journal:

> . . . we want. . . . Survival gives. . . . We exam-
> ine. . . . We compare. . . . We have used. . . . Each has
> been weighted. . . . We merely take. . . . They are sub-
> ject. . . . We use . . . Efron and Morris (3) describe. . . .
> We observed. . . . We might find. . . . We know. . . .
> Averages for a season ordinarily run. . . . Spread
> comes. . . . We can shrink. . . . How this is done is
> explained. . . . The explanation is given. . . .
>
> —John P. Gilbert, Bucknam McPeek, and Frederick Mosteller,
> "Statistics and Ethics in Surgery and Anesthesia," *Science*

This prejudice against first-person writing is as deeply rooted in the academic mentality as it is mistaken. Here are two versions of the same content, one passive and thick with nominalizations, the other active and alive with verbs:

> It has been stated that the assessment of the mobility of the
> detached retina is a factor when the nondrainage retinal
> detachment operation of Custodis and Lincoff is being given
> consideration. Determination of the mobility of the de-
> tached retina is made on the basis of two factors. The depth
> of the subretinal fluid is the first to be given consideration.
> If the subretinal fluid is shallow, then little room is given for
> actual movement of the detached retina.

> Several researchers have stated that when we consider the
> Custodis-Lincoff operation, in which we do not drain the
> retina, we must first assess how mobile the detached retina
> is. We can determine its mobility in two ways. First, how
> deep is the subretinal fluid? If it is shallow, then the de-
> tached retina has little room in which to move.

The active-verbal version sounds more prosaic, less academic, the passive-nominal version appropriately scientific. But given the choice, who would choose to slog through page after page of that academic obscurity?

Every profession demands from its apprentices its own peculiar tone of voice, the special accent that testifies that a writer is familiar with and accepts the implicit values which define that profession. A writer must learn not only to act like a professional but to sound like one as well. It is profoundly unfortunate for us all, but most acutely for the public at large, that the tone most academics assume—mindlessly or deliberately—makes their prose so resolutely inaccessible.

To be sure, we would find most professional prose difficult even if its style were always clear. To understand advanced work in any field requires that we possess its special knowledge, control its technical vocabulary, and understand the nuances of particular forms of argument. But when these problems of local competence conspire with the general problem of a turgidly complex prose style, it becomes difficult, if not virtually impossible, for the merely educated and intelligent layperson to appreciate even the outlines of issues and arguments important not just to a special field, but often to society in general.

Exercise 1–2

Clarify these passages. Change passives into actives only where you can improve the sentence. If necessary, invent a rhetorical situation to explain your choice.

1. Your figures have been reanalyzed in order to determine the coefficient of error. The results will be announced when the situation is judged appropriate.
2. Almost all home mortgage loans nowadays are made for twenty-five to thirty years. With the price of housing at such inflated levels, those loans cannot be paid off in any shorter period of time.
3. Trotsky's usual impassioned narrative style is abandoned and in its place a cautious and scholarly treatment of theories of conspiracy is presented. But the moment the narrative line is picked up again, he invests his prose with the same vigor and force.
4. Many arguments have been advanced against Darwinian evolution because basic assumptions about our place in the world were contradicted by it. No longer was man seen as the privileged creature in God's Great Scheme of Things but rather as an accidental consequence of natural forces.
5. For many years federal regulations concerning the use of wiretapping have been regularly ignored. Only recently have tighter restrictions been imposed on the circumstances that warrant it.

In these next sentences, change passives to actives and edit nominalizations into a more direct agent-action style. Again, invent agents where necessary.

6. It is my belief that the social significance of Restoration comedy can be provided with the clearest explanation through an analysis of social relationships portrayed in the plays. In particular, studies can be made of the manner in which interactions between different social levels are conducted.

7. These technical directives are written in a style of maximum simplicity as a result of an attempt at more effective communication with employees of little education who have been hired in accordance with guidelines that have been imposed.

8. The participants received information that they would be reimbursed, but a decision has been made that such an action cannot be accomplished at this time.

9. The tissue rejection evaluation was performed according to procedures that have been abandoned because of their consistent overestimation of antibody production values.

10. The ability of the human brain to arrive at solutions of human problems has been universally undervalued, because research has not been done that would be considered to have scientific reliability.

NOUN + NOUN + NOUN

Like the passive, another habit of style that will prevent you from linking one idea to another clearly and explicitly is the long compound noun phrase. It is a habit especially popular among scholarly and technical writers:

> *Early childhood thought disorder misdiagnosis* often occurs as a result of unfamiliarity with recent *research literature* describing such conditions. This paper is a review of seven recent studies in which are findings of particular relevance to *preteen hyperactivity diagnosis* and to *treatment modalities* involving *medication maintenance level evaluation procedures.*

Some grammarians insist that we should never modify one noun with another, but such a rule would keep us from using such common phrases as *stone wall, student committee,* and *radio telescope.* We can more persuasively reject such phrases on the grounds that most of them are awkward or, worse, ambiguous, especially when they include nominalizations. They may seem more economical than the fully articulated phrase, and they may be entirely acceptable in scientific and technical writing. But they are graceless all the same. And when we recognize their potential ambiguity, we may decide that the very slight economy is a bad bargain.

Whenever you find in your writing a string of consecutive nouns, try unpacking them. Start from the last noun and reverse their order, rewriting the string into explicit prepositional phrases. If one of the nouns is a nominalization, rewrite it into a full verb. For example, here is the first compound noun phrase in the sample paragraph above:

1   2   3   4
early childhood thought disorder misdiagnosis
4   3   2   1
misdiagnosis disorder thought childhood

(At this point we can see where the ambiguity lies: What's early, the childhood, the disorder, or the diagnosis?) Now rewrite the string into a full phrase, using a verb if you can:

misdiagnose disordered thought in childhood

If we unpack the other phrases and then reassemble them into a complete sentence, we get something a bit clearer:

Physicians are misdiagnosing disordered thought in young children because they are unfamiliar with the literature on recent research.

You can lighten the rhythm of a sentence if you also watch for possessive nouns, nouns that have an apostrophe in them:

The city's *sales tax position* toward an increase contradicts **the State Finance Office's** *recent announcement.*

You can translate most possessive nouns into prepositional phrases:

> The position *of* the city toward a sales tax increase contradicts a recent announcement *from* the State Finance Office.

Don't apply this advice to human or animal possessive nouns. For some reason, they don't burden a sentence the way nonhuman possessives do:

> The *President's intention* to reach an agreement with the Soviet Union on Afghanistan depends on Senator Byrd's *support.*

Exercise 1–3

Turn the compound noun phrases in 1–5 into prepositional phrases.

1. The plant safety standards committee discussed recent air quality regulation announcements.
2. Diabetic patient blood pressure reduction may be a consequence of renal extract depressor agent application.
3. Pancreatic gland motor phenomena are regulated chiefly by parasympathetic nervous system cells.
4. The main goal of this article is to describe text comprehension processes and recall protocol production.
5. On the basis of these principles, we may now attempt to formulate narrative information extraction rules.

In these next sentences, unpack compound nouns, and edit the indirect style by placing agents and actions in subjects and verbs. Invent agents where necessary.

6. This paper is an investigation into information processing behavior involved in computer human cognition simulation games.
7. Enforcement of guidelines for new car model tire durability is a Federal Trade Commission responsibility.
8 . Upon court appearance by the defendant, courtroom legal service will be effected by the presiding justice with the request for time requirement waiver so that the case hearing can begin.

9. The Social Security program is a standard monthly income floor guarantee for individuals whose benefit package potential is based on a determination of lifelong contribution schedule.

10. Based on extensive training needs assessment reviews and on selected CETA office site visits, there was the identification of concepts and issues to constitute an initial staff questionnaire instrument.

11. Corporation organization under state law supervision has resulted in federal government inability as to effective implementation of pollution reduction measures.

12. Determination of support appropriateness for community organization assistance need was precluded by difficulty in the obtaining of data relevant to a committee activity review.

13. The secretary of the Department of Energy's November 1, 1979, press release announcement was to the effect that there was a decision for surplus alcohol stock disposal on the part of major manufacturers as a result of the October 28 meeting discussions between the manufacturers and the DOE.

14. The existence of these aforementioned conditions in regard to improper reimbursement claims is due to compliance failure of relevant school personnel and to student reimbursement claim reviews being ineffective or inadequate.

15. The art of cardiac sound interpretation requires an intimate cardiac physiology and cardiac disease pathophysiology knowledge.

SUMMING UP

The Essentials of Clarity

Nominalizations, passives, missing agents, compound noun phrases—they all keep us from fully using those resources of an English sentence that help us express clearly and exactly the meaning we intend. Here are some guidelines.

1.   Whenever you can, use specific verbs, adverbs, or adjectives rather than abstract nouns to express actions and conditions:

> The **intention** of the committee is the **improvement** of company morale.

> The committee **intends** to **improve** company morale.

2.   When it is appropriate, make the subjects of your verbs the agents of those actions:

> A decision on the part of **the Dean** in regard to the funding by **the Department** of the program must be made for there to be adequate **staff** preparation.

> **The Dean** must decide whether **the Department** will fund the program if **the staff** is to prepare adequately.

3.   Avoid making up new compound noun phrases. Use verbs, adjectives, and prepositional phrases:

> **Administration overrun anticipation capability reviews** are being instituted to prevent **surprise military equipment cost prediction problems.**

> The Administration is reviewing how well it can anticipate overruns so that it will not be surprised by problems with predicting the cost of military equipment.

4.   Do not waste time trying to rewrite passives into actives when the agent of the action is unknown or unimportant:

> The President **was re-elected** with 54% of the vote.

5.   Do not waste time trying to rewrite nominalizations back into verbs if the nominalization sums up what went before:

> **Analyses of this kind** invariably produce misleading results.

The Grammar of Coherence

Well begun is half done.

ANONYMOUS

The two capital secrets in the art of prose composition are these: first the philosophy of transition and connection; or the art by which one step in an evolution of thought is made to arise out of another: all fluent and effective composition depends on the connections; secondly, the way in which sentences are made to modify each other; for the most powerful effects in written eloquence arise out of this reverberation, as it were, from each other in a rapid succession of sentences.

THOMAS DE QUINCEY

"Begin at the beginning," the King said, gravely, "and go on till you come to the end; then stop."

LEWIS CARROLL

S|o far, we've talked about clear and direct writing as if we wrote only individual sentences*, independent of any larger context or governing intention; as if the form of a sentence stood in some fixed and predictable ideal relationship to the ideas it expressed. And it's true that by arranging agents and actions to fit subjects* and verbs*, we can achieve a kind of local clarity. But if we don't design those individually clear sentences to emphasize our most important ideas, if we don't make those sentences fit the context of the sentences around them, then no matter how clear they may be, they won't add up to cohesive discourse.

The problem we want to address in this Lesson and the next is how, without sacrificing clarity, we can shape sentences to communicate ideas in ways that are appropriate to our context and to our intended emphasis.

CONTEXTS

One of the facts that makes English such a rich complex instrument of expression is that in some sentences our optimally clear and direct order of

subject*	verb*	object*
agent*	action*	goal*

may not be the best order if we also want to be appropriately emphatic and cohesive. For example, few principles of style are more widely invoked than the one that calls for using the direct and vigorous active* rather than the indirect passive*. Not

> A black hole *is created* by the collapse of a dead star into a point perhaps no larger than a marble.

but

> The collapse of a dead star into a point perhaps no larger than a marble *creates* a black hole.

But suppose the context for the sentence was this:

> Some astonishing questions about the nature of the universe
> have been raised by scientists exploring the nature of black
> holes in space. . . . So much matter compressed into so lit-
> tle volume changes the fabric of space around it in pro-
> foundly astonishing ways.

Our sense of coherence and rhythm should tell us that this context calls not for the active, but for the passive. And the reasons are not far to seek: The last part of the first sentence, *the nature of black holes in space,* introduces words that in the second sentence would be the object* of an active verb.

> . . . collapse creates *a black hole.*

But we would improve the transition between the first and second sentences if we could shift that object to the beginning of its own sentence, closer to the end of the previous sentence. And we can do that by making it the subject of a passive verb:

> . . . the nature of *black holes in space.* A *black hole* is created
> when . . .

The problem—and the challenge—of English prose is that in almost every sentence we write, we have to strike the best compromise among the principles of clarity and directness that we discussed in the first Lesson, the emphasis we intend, and those principles of coherence and cohesion that fuse separate sentences into a whole discourse. *But in that compromise, we must always give priority to emphasis and cohesion, to what fuses sentences into cohesive discourse.*

There are two complementary principles of order and emphasis. We've just illustrated one of them:

> *Whenever possible, express at the beginning of a sentence ideas
> already stated, referred to, implied, safely assumed, familiar,
> predictable, less important, readily accessible information.*

The other principle is this:

> *Express at the end of a sentence the least predictable, the newest, the most important, the most significant information, the information you almost certainly want to emphasize.*

In short, as you begin a sentence, prepare the reader for the new or important information you want to communicate. Give the reader a context to move from the known to the unknown, from the predictable to the unpredictable.

BEGINNING WELL

It's more difficult to begin a sentence well than to end it well. As we'll see later, to end a sentence well, we need only decide which idea is the newest, the most important. It probably will be the idea we want to emphasize, often the one we'll expand on in the next sentence. We just put that idea at the end of its sentence.

But every time we begin a new sentence, we may have to manage three or four elements that we typically open with. And since what we put at the beginning of a sentence strongly determines how the reader understands what follows, we have to be especially careful to start each sentence off in the right way. When we begin a sentence, we have to manage all of this:

1. To connect the new sentence to the preceding one, we use cohesive and transitional devices such as *and, but, therefore, as a result.*
2. We tell our readers how to evaluate what follows with expressions such as *fortunately, perhaps, allegedly, it is important to note that.*
3. We orient our reader to what follows with some preliminary context: *for the most part, in many ways, under these circumstances, to a certain extent, from a practical point of view, politically speaking.*
4. We typically set the time and place of an action: *at that time, later, on May 23, in Europe.*
5. And most importantly (note the evaluation), we announce the *topic** of a sentence, either by naming it in the subject of a clause* or by introducing it with phrases such as *in regard to, as for, turning now to, as far as X is concerned.*

Topics

The topic of a sentence or clause is what you announce that sentence or clause is about, what the rest of the sentence comments on. In most sentences, the topic is the subject:

> *Private higher education* is seriously concerned about population trends through the end of the century.

But you can make an object a topic if you shift that object to the beginning of its sentence, before the subject:

> I cannot now explore *the reasons for this decision.*
> *The reasons for this decision* I cannot now explore.

You can also put topics in introductory phrases:

> In regard to *abortion,* few issues have so excited the passions of supporters and opponents alike.

> About the *religious cults* that capture the minds of young people, what is there to say except that they must be recognized for what they are: destructive movements that prey on the insecurities of confused adolescents.

Ordinarily, though, the topics of your sentences are their subjects.

In this paragraph, *the topics* are italicized: *Topics* are crucial because *they* focus a reader's attention on particular ideas toward the beginning of each clause. Cumulatively, *these ideas* provide thematic signposts that should focus your reader's attention toward a well-defined set of connected ideas. If a *sequence of topics* seems coherent, they will move the reader through a paragraph from a cumulatively coherent point of view. But if through that paragraph *the topics* shift randomly, then *your reader* has to begin each sentence out of context, from no coherent point of view. *Whatever you announce as a topic,* then, will fix your reader's point of view, not just toward the rest of the sentence, but toward sequences of sentences, toward whole chunks of discourse.

Compare this:

> In this next paragraph, *italics* mark topics: *Particular ideas toward the beginning of each clause* focus the reader's attention, so *topics* are crucial. Cumulatively, *thematic*

signposts that are provided by these ideas should focus the reader's attention toward a well-defined set of connected ideas. *Moving through a paragraph from a cumulatively coherent point of view* is made possible by a sequence of topics that seem to constitute a coherent sequence of connected ideas. *A lack of context for each sentence* is one consequence of making the reader begin sentences with random shifts in topics. *The rest of the sentence as well as whole chunks of discourse* will be the objects of a reader's point of view as a result of topic announcement.

Compare the sequences of topics in the original and this revised paragraph

Original	**Revised**
the topics	italics
Topics	particular ideas toward the beginning of each clause
they (topics)	topics
these ideas	thematic signposts . . . for us
a sequence of topics	Moving through a paragraph from a cumulatively coherent point of view
we	A lack of context for each sentence
the topics	The sentence . . . chunks of discourse
our reader	
Whatever we announce as a topic	

The original focuses on only two topics: *topics* and *reader*. The revised has no consistent focus.

This principle of a coherent sequence of topics should also explain why one long sentence after another can be cumulatively so confusing. Very long sentences don't let you clearly announce topics often enough to guide your reader through a multitude of ideas. Readers need thematic signposts to help them assemble the ideas in individual sentences and clauses into coherent and cohesive discourse.

And this reinforces the point we made about agents and actions: When you consistently arrange your sentences so that their subjects are agents and their verbs are actions, you are beginning your sentences from a consistent point of view, from the point of view of agency. As we are going to see, most of the principles of clear writing that we will be working through fit together like this into a coherent *system* of principles, one principle reinforcing another.

Now at this point, some of you may be recalling advice that you once received about how to avoid "monotony." You may have been told to vary the way you begin your sentences, to avoid beginning your sentences with the same subjects.

That's bad advice.

Your prose will become monotonous for reasons more serious than repeating topics or subjects. It will be monotonous if you write one short sentence after another, or one long sentence after another. It will be monotonous if you stuff it full of abstract nominalizations and passives. The way to avoid monotony is to say what you have to say as clearly as you can. If that means you have to make the subjects of several consecutive sentences the agents of crucial actions, take heart: Your prose will then be both clear and cohesive. At the risk of asking a question that might invite a wrong answer, did the original paragraph about topics, the first one with the italicized topics, seem monotonous? It has only two topics: *topics* and *reader*. If, as you read that paragraph, your eyes did not glaze over, then we have settled the issue of monotony and consistent topics.

Furthermore, if you attend to this principle of ordering old information before new information, you will probably avoid another problem—subjects that are necessarily long and diffuse just because they are presenting new information. Look again at the string of topics in our pair of paragraphs about topics. In the revised version, the subjects/topics are long and complex, partly because they express newer ideas. In the original, on the other hand, the subjects/topics are short, concise and specific. Because the topics expressed familiar information, we were able to phrase them in a few words, or even a single pronoun*. If the topics of your sentences refer to ideas you have already mentioned, your subjects will be consistently short and precise, closely connected to your verbs. And that will get your sentences off to a brisk start.

Incidentally, there are good psychological reasons for this old/new, short/long principle of style. The first is that when we want to communicate a new idea, we do well to associate it with something our reader already knows. That applies to a whole body of material as well as to a single sentence. The second good reason is that as soon as a reader begins reading a subject, that reader begins looking for the verb that goes with it. If over and over, the reader has to unscramble a long subject and at the same time watch for that verb, he's going to lose track of the sentence. And if sentence after sentence begins that way, then your reader will lose the focus of whole paragraphs.

MANAGING SUBJECTS

English provides a number of ways to make a long subject shorter, usually by switching it with another, shorter part of the sentence, a part that is probably shorter because it contains repeated information. Notice that in each of the following sentences, we move to the end a long subject that expresses the important, usually new information. Note too that the shorter segment we move to the beginning usually expresses older information, information that connects with something that has gone before.

1. Passives again. One important use of the passive is that it lets us switch a long subject full of new information for a short one that repeats something already mentioned or relatively more familiar:

   During the first years of our Republic, *a series of brilliant and virtuous presidents committed to a democracy yet confident in their own special competence* conducted **its administration.**
   During the first years of our Republic, **its administration** was conducted *by a series of brilliant and virtuous presidents committed to a democracy yet confident in their own special competence.*

   Astronomers, physicists, and a host of other researchers entirely familiar with the problems raised by quasars have confirmed **these observations.**
   These observations have been confirmed by *astronomers, physicists, and a host of other researchers entirely familiar with the problems raised by quasars.*

The passive exists largely for just this function—to re-arrange a sentence to improve cohesion and emphasis. Most textbooks simply tell us to avoid them on general principle. That's more bad advice.

2. Subject-complement* switching. Sometimes, we can simply switch the subject and complement, especially when what follows the linking verb *be* refers to something already mentioned:

> *The source of the American attitude toward rural dialects* is **more interesting** (than something already mentioned.)
> **More interesting** (than something already mentioned) is *the source of the American attitude toward rural dialects.*

We can make a similar switch with a few other verbs:

> *The failure of the administration to halt the continually rising costs of hospital care* lies **at the heart of the problem.**
> **At the heart of the problem** lies *the failure of the administration to halt the continually rising costs of hospital care.*

> *Some very difficult theoretical issues* run **through these questions.**
> **Through these questions** run *some very difficult theoretical issues.*

Here are the two principles that are more important than always getting agents into the subjects of your sentences:

1. Put in the subject/topic of your sentences ideas that you have already mentioned, or ideas that are so familiar to your reader that your mentioning them at the beginning of a sentence will not seem abrupt.
2. Keep your topics consistent. That doesn't mean they have to be identical. But they should be a group of words and phrases that constitute a coherent and consistent set.

Here are two consequences of following that advice:

1. You may find yourself writing more passive than active sentences. If so, try revising them into their active form. But if the result is a less consistent sequence of topics, leave the sentences passive.

2. As noted in Lesson One, you may find yourself using nominalizations* as topics because those nominalizations refer to ideas in sentences that went before. That is one important function of nominalizations: to sum up in one phrase actions you have just mentioned so that you can comment on them.

> In order to account for the complex relationships among colonies of genetically related samples, it is necessary to track the genetic history through several hundred generations. *This kind of investigation* requires that we keep exceptionally careful histories of all members in the field.

Sentences that express ideas in agent/subject-action/verb sequences will usually be clearer than sentences that don't. But that principle of style must always yield to one that makes for cohesiveness: old information first—new information last.

Once we understand why it's important to create a consistent string of appropriate topics, we also understand why it's important to manage all those other elements that we also usually put at the beginning of a sentence. We have to make sure they don't obscure or confuse those topics.

TRANSITION

There's no consensus among editors and writers on how best to use words that connect sentences, words like *therefore, however, nevertheless,* and *but, yet, so.* Some editors suggest that we should use many of them; others, few. Some competent writers use them frequently, others rarely. But however you use them, put them close to the beginning of their sentences, usually among the first six words. Here are some common transitional devices:

— *Adding:* furthermore, in addition, moreover, similarly, and, also
— *Opposing:* but, however, though, nevertheless, on the other hand
— *Concluding:* so, therefore, for, as a result, consequently
— *Exemplifying:* for example, for instance, to illustrate, that is

— *Intensifying:* in fact, indeed, even, as a matter of fact
— *Sequencing:* first, second, finally, in conclusion, to sum up

Adding: If you begin a sentence or a paragraph with *also, and,* or *another,* look closely. You do nothing intrinsically wrong by starting with *and,* but general connectors like these suggest that you may not have thought through the exact logical connections between your ideas, that you may be just adding one thought to another. *Also* at the beginning of a sentence can make it seem especially tacked-on:

> Metaphor is one of the most difficult figures of speech for an inexperienced writer to master. *Also,* irony can be a problem.

Be sure your *also* introduces a second item parallel to the preceding one, not an elaboration on the first:

> Metaphor is one of the most difficult figures of speech for an inexperienced writer to master. Also, it requires a mature imagination and a sense of appropriateness.

That *also* doesn't introduce something parallel to metaphor, but something that elaborates on it. *Because* would be more exact:

> . . . an inexperienced writer to master, *because* it requires a mature imagination and a sense of appropriateness.

And avoid beginning more than a few sentences with *and*: Reserve it for places where you want some special emphasis, usually at the end of a sequence of points. You can use it to signal your reader that you have come to the last item in a series.

Opposing: Whenever you contradict or qualify a statement, signal that qualification early on with *but, however, on the other hand.* A sequence of *buts* can be both confusing and awkward:

> The competition to discover the particular shape of the DNA chain come down to what looked like a dead heat between Linus Pauling and the Watson-Crick team, *but* it was the lat-

ter who had the decided advantage of far superior X-ray photographs. *But* even if Pauling had had the same pictures, he probably wouldn't have been able to look at them objectively so committed was he to the concept of a triple helix.

You can avoid a second *but* with a *however:*

The competition to discover the particular shape of the DNA chain came down to what looked like a dead heat between Linus Pauling and the Watson-Crick team. Even if Pauling had had the same pictures, however, he probably wouldn't have been able to. . . .

You can also change that second *but* to a *though* and move it into its sentence a word or two:

The competition to discover the particular shape of the DNA chain came down to what looked like a dead heat between Linus Pauling and the Watson-Crick team, but it was the latter who had the decided advantage of far superior X-ray photographs. Even if Pauling had had the same pictures, *though,* he probably wouldn't have been able. . . .

Concluding: Use logical connectors such as *therefore, hence, thus* and *then* sparingly. Your ideas should flow clearly enough not to need them, except for special emphasis. Because they are so varied, it might be useful to review their exact meanings:

— *As a result:* The final consequence in a chain of events.
— *Consequently:* A peripheral or direct result but not necessarily the final one.
— *Therefore:* Introduces a step in a logical sequence, not in a causal one.
— *Thus, hence, then:* Close to *therefore.*
— *So:* Less formal than the others, and because it is less specific, it can replace most of them in a casual style.

Examples:

The appreciation of the dollar against the mark has made German imports increasingly inexpensive. *As a result,* products ranging from wine to automobiles are coming into the range of the middle-class American market.

New right-to-privacy laws have made it impossible to compile health data in the ways we have been doing it. *Consequently,* we are no longer able to analyze the real needs of our students.

Your application failed to indicate the financial resources of your family. We must *therefore* reject your application for scholarship aid.

ORIENTERS

Orienters guide a reader through a sentence by establishing a point of view toward what they introduce. They may set the time or place of events:

During the next few years, America must solve its balance of payments problem.
In many parts of the globe, life is as short and brutal as it was during prehistoric times.

Orienters can also restrict the range or certainty of an assertion:

Under certain circumstances, it is possible to control one's autonomic nervous system.
Up to a point, we are all willing to follow orders without question.

And they can state how something should be understood:

From a political point of view, the President's efforts to bring peace to the Middle East were at best a risky undertaking.
Pragmatically, we would do better to make the package smaller and the price higher.

Because orienters provide the context for an assertion, they are most helpful early in the sentence. When indicators of time and degree, of point of view and cohesion, appear at the end of a sentence, they force a reader to re-orient retrospectively.

Exercise 2–1

In the following units, edit to improve cohesive flow. (1) Move transitional devices and orienters to the beginning of their sentences; (2) arrange the order of topics so that they are logical. Generally edit the passages so that they are more economical and direct.

1. Analytic and normative criticism are the two modes that this kind of stylistic criticism comes in. That the best of all possible texts for the content it expresses is the text before us is the assumption of analytic criticism. To explain why the text is as it is is the only task of the analytic critic. Where the writer missed matching his language to his ideas is explained by the normative critic, on the other hand. That the writer could have failed to achieve his intention is its assumption. The fame or obscurity of the author more than the intrinsic quality of a text determines which we choose.

2. A steady Darwinian selection has been imposed on the population of discontented Europeans by the discovery of America. A new chance to come here made the most intrepid and least rooted gladly give up everything. Staying put was the lot of the lazy, the fearful, the least discontented. Personality traits that led to an adventurous independence have always been favored by the gene pool that has constituted the American genetic heritage, as a result.

3. Vegetation covers the earth, except for those areas continuously covered with ice or utterly scorched by continual heat. Richly fertilized plains and river valleys are places where plants grow, as well as at the edge of perpetual snow in high mountains. There is plant growth not only in and around lakes and swamps but under the ocean and next to it. The cracks of busy city sidewalks have plants in them as well as in barren rocks. Before man existed the earth was covered with vegetation, and the earth will have vegetation long after evolutionary history swallows us up.

4. The power to create and communicate a new message to fit a new experience is not part of the power of animals in their natural states. Their genetic code imposes on them only what they can communicate. Information in regard to distance,

direction, source richness, in regard to pollen, constitutes the total information content which can be communicated by bees. The same limited repertoire of messages delivered over and over in the same way, for generation after generation, is characteristic of animals of the same species, in all significant respects, however.

THE NUANCES OF CONTROLLING YOUR TOPIC

It's possible to create very subtle effects in your prose if you find verbs that let you shift into your subject/topic position just those words that will allow you to control your audience's point of view. Here, for example, are the first few sentences of Lincoln's Gettysburg Address, written from a different topical point of view:

> Four score and seven years ago, *this continent* witnessed the birth of a new nation, conceived in liberty and dedicated by our fathers to the proposition that all men are created equal. Now, a *great Civil War* engages us, testing whether that nation or any nation so conceived and so dedicated, can long endure. *That War* has provided us with a great battlefield for this our meeting place. *A portion of this field* is to receive our dedication as the final resting place for those who here gave their lives that this nation might live. *This* is altogether a fitting and proper thing to do. But in a larger sense, *this ground* will not let us dedicate, consecrate, or hallow it. *It* has received that consecration from the brave men, living and dead, who struggled here, far above our poor power to add or detract. *What is said here* will be little noted nor long remembered, but *what those men did here* can never be forgotten.

Compare with the original:

> Four score and seven years ago *our fathers* brought forth on this continent a new nation, conceived in liberty, and dedicated to the proposition that all men are created equal.
>
> Now *we* are engaged in a great civil war, testing whether *that nation,* or any nation so conceived and so dedicated, can long endure. *We* are met on a great battlefield of that war. *We* have come to dedicate a portion of that field as a

final resting place for *those who* here gave their lives that *that nation* might live. It is altogether fitting and proper that *we* should do this. [Everything before the *we* is introductory. See metadiscourse* in Lesson Three.]

But, in a larger sense, *we* cannot dedicate—*we* cannot consecrate—*we* cannot hallow this ground. *The brave men,* living and dead, who struggled here have consecrated it, far above our poor power to add or detract. *The world* will little note, nor long remember what *we* say here, but *it* can never forget what *they* did here. It is for *us the living,* rather, to be dedicated here to the unfinished work which *they who* fought here have thus far so nobly advanced. It is rather for *us* to be here dedicated to the great task remaining before us—that from these honored dead *we* take increased devotion to that cause for which *they* gave the last full measure of devotion—that *we* here highly resolve that *these dead* shall not have died in vain—that *this nation,* under God, shall have a new birth of freedom—and that *government of the people, by the people, and for the people,* shall not perish from the earth.

In the original Lincoln made his subject/agent/topics these (I have added the verbs to give the topics some context):

Topics	Predicate
our fathers	brought forth
we	are engaged
that nation	can long endure
we	are met
we	have come
those who	here gave
we	do this
we	cannot dedicate
we	cannot consecrate
we	cannot hallow
the brave men	have consecrated it
the world	will little note
it (the world)	can never forget
they	did

The topics of the revision are quite different, but still consistent: they are the locations of the actions or the actions themselves metaphorically transformed into seeming agents.

this continent	witnessed
a great civil war	engages us
That War	has provided us
a portion of this field	is to receive
this	is altogether a fitting
this ground	will not let us
It	has received
what is said here	will be little noted
what those men did here	can never be forgotten

What's the difference? In his speech, Lincoln has assigned responsibility to his audience. By making them the agents of the actions, he has identified them with the founding fathers and with the men who fought and died at Gettysburg. By so doing, he has tacitly invited his listeners to identify with the great sacrifices still necessary to preserve a government of the people, by the people, and for the people.

My revision, on the other hand, metaphorically shifts agency away from people to abstractions and places: the continent witnesses, a great civil war engages, the war provides, a portion of the field receives, etc. I have retold Lincoln's story from a different point of view, metaphorically investing agency and responsibility in a different set of entities. Had Lincoln written my version, he would have relieved his audience of its profound responsibility to act, and would thereby have deprived us of the greatest speech in American history.

We have to be wary, though, to know when these metaphors become not our servants, but our masters. Sometimes, abstractions seem to take on a power independent of human agency.

> The evidence demands that the earlier decisions continue to guide our planning. The present need for further cutbacks clearly demonstrates the wisdom of this course of action.

When *evidence demands* and *decisions guide,* when *a need demonstrates,* we want to be sure we have not put ourselves at the mercy of our own abstractions.

Exercise 2–2

1. At the beginning of this passage from his essay, "Stranger in the Village," James Baldwin makes the cathedral at Chartres the topic and metaphorical agency of the sentence. But then he makes the villagers and himself topics. Rewrite this passage so that in the first sentence the villagers and Baldwin are the topics/subjects/agents. What difference does it make? What other changes of this kind—shifting senses of agency and topic—can you make? What consequences do they have?

   > The cathedral at Chartres, I have said, says something to the people of this village which it cannot say to me; but it is important to understand that this cathedral says something to me which it cannot say to them. Perhaps they are struck by the power of the spires, the glory of the windows; but they have known God, after all, longer than I have known him, and in a different way, and I am terrified by the slippery bottomless well to be found in the crypt, down which heretics were hurled to death, and by the obscene, inescapable gargoyles jutting out of the stone and seeming to say that God and the devil can never be divorced. I doubt that the villagers think of the devil when they face a cathedral because they have never been identified with the devil. But I must accept the status which myth, if nothing else, gives me in the West before I can hope to change the myth.

2. Revise this passage by the American historian, Frederick Turner, so that the topics of the sentences constitute a different but consistent set of topics/agents/subjects. For example, the first sentence could read,

   > The colonist must submit to the wilderness.

   Why is it appropriate that at the beginning of the passage, Turner made the wilderness the seeming agency, but that toward the end, he assigned agency to the colonists?

   > The wilderness masters the colonist. It finds him a European in dress, industries, tools, modes of travel and thought. It

takes him from the railroad car and puts him in the birch
canoe. It strips off the garments of civilization and arrays
him in the hunting shirt and the moccasin. It puts him in the
log cabin of the Cherokee and the Iroquois and runs an Indian palisade around him. Before long, he has gone to
planting Indian corn and ploughing with a sharp stick: he
shouts the war-cry and takes the scalp in orthodox Indian
fashion. In short, the frontier is at first too strong for the
man. He must accept the conditions which it furnishes, or
perish, and so he fits himself into the Indian clearings and
follows the Indian trails. Little by little he overcomes the
wilderness, but the outcome is not the old Europe. The fact
is, that here is a new product that is American.

SUMMING UP

1. As a general principle, use the beginning of your sentences to
   refer to
   a. what you have already mentioned,
   b. knowledge that you can assume you and your reader
      readily share.

Not:

> The huge number of wounded and dead in *the Civil War*
> exceeded all the *other wars in American history.* One of the
> reasons for the lingering animosity between North and
> South today is *the memory of this terrible carnage.*

But:

> Of *all the wars in American history,* none has exceeded *the
> Civil War* in the huge number of wounded and dead. *The
> memory of this terrible carnage* is one of the reasons for the
> animosity between North and South today.

2. Put transitional words such as *therefore, on the other hand,
   of course,* close to the beginning of your sentences.

Not:

> The memory of this terrible carnage is one of the reasons
> for the animosity between North and South today. This cen-
> tury old hostility is manifested in ways that are often in-
> direct, and therefore often misunderstood, *however.*

But:

> The memory of this terrible carnage is one of the reasons
> for the animosity between North and South today. *However,*
> this century old hostility is manifested in ways that are often
> indirect and therefore, often misunderstood.

3. Put orienting words and phrases such as *for the most part,
   economically speaking, in the early part of the Christian era,*
   at the beginning of your sentences. Make them as short as you
   can.

Not:

> We may project particular latent attitudes that we have been
> taught onto certain traits of culture and personality that we
> believe characterize the other, *depending on our
> background.*

But:

> *Depending on our background,* we may project particular
> latent attitudes we have been taught onto certain traits of
> culture and personality that we believe characterize the
> other.

4. Ask yourself whether the topics you have chosen control your
   reader's point of view in the way that will be most useful to
   you. Which of these would better serve the needs of a patient
   suing a physician is obvious:

> A patient whose reactions go unmonitored may also claim
> physician liability. In this case, a patient took Cloromax as
> prescribed, which resulted in partial renal failure. The
> manufacturer's literature indicated that the patient should be
> observed frequently and should immediately report any sign

of infection. Evidence indicated that the patient had not received instructions to report any signs of urinary blockage. Furthermore, the patient had no white cell count taken until after he developed the blockage.

If a physician does not monitor his patient's reactions, he may be held liable. In this case, the physician prescribed Cloromax, which caused the patient to experience partial renal failure. The physician had been cautioned by the manufacturer's literature that he should observe the patient frequently and instruct the patient to report any sign of infection. Evidence indicates that the physician did not instruct the patient to report any sign of urinary blockage. Furthermore, he made no white cell count until after the patient developed the blockage.

The general principle is this:

topic		stress
old		new
subject	verb	complement
agent	action	verb

The Grammar of Emphasis

All's well that ends well.

WILLIAM SHAKESPEARE

In the end is my beginning.

T. S. ELIOT

If you begin a sentence well, the end will almost take care of itself. If at the beginning of your sentences, you have announced as topics those ideas that you want to say something about, especially those ideas you have already mentioned, then almost by default you will have to put at the *end* of your sentences new and therefore more important information. If you do not manage the flow of your ideas in this way, your prose will seem not just unfocused, but weak, anticlimactic.

Because the beginning of a sentence serves so crucial a role, we found a name for it: *topic.* The end of a sentence is no less important. We could use a name for it as well. When you utter a sentence, your voice rises and falls. When you approach a major break in the flow of words, particularly near the end, you ordinarily raise your pitch on one of those last few words and stress it just a bit more strongly than the others:

                                        o
. . . a bit more strongly than the
                                           thers.

The natural rhythm, pitch and stress of our voices signal the end of a sentence more prominently than they signal any other part. We'll call that part of a sentence leading up to and including this most strongly emphasized part of a sentence, the *stress.*

MANAGING ENDINGS

You can manage the information in this stressed part of the sentence in a number of ways. You can, of course, put your newest and most important information there in the first place. Often, though, even the best writers have to edit their sentences to get that information under the right emphasis.

1. Trim the end.

One way to do that is to move less important phrases and clauses *away* from the end of a sentence, so that you leave exposed at the end what you want to emphasize:

> The data that are offered to establish the existence of ESP do not make believers of us *for the most part.*

> *For the most part,* the data that are offered to establish the existence of ESP do not make believers of us.

Occasionally, this principle overrides the general principle of not separating subjects from verbs or verbs from objects. This sentence ends weakly:

No one can explain why that first primeval superatom exploded and thereby created the universe in a few words.

The object of *explain,* the clause *why that first primeval superatom exploded and thereby created the universe,* is much longer than *in a few words,* the modifier of *explain.* We can create a smoother flow if we put that shorter, less important modifier before the longer, more important object, even if we have to split the object from its verb:

No one can explain *in a few words* why that first primeval superatom exploded and thereby created the universe.

In other cases, we can simply lop off final unnecessary words and phrases until we get to the information we want to stress, leaving that information in the final position.

Sociobiologists are making the provocative claim that our genes largely determine our social behavior in the way we act in situations we find around us every day.

Since social behavior means the way we act, we can just drop everything after *behavior:*

Social biologists are making the provocative claim that our genes largely determine our social behavior.

2.   Shift a chunk to the right.

Moving the important information *to* the end of the sentence is another way to manage the flow of ideas. And the sentence you just read illustrates a missed opportunity. This version is more cohesive and emphatic:

Another way *to* manage the flow of ideas is by moving the most important information to the end of the sentence.

In fact, this is just the other side of something we've already seen—how to move old information to the beginning of a sentence. Sentences that introduce a paragraph or a new section of a paper are frequently of an *X is Y* form. One part, usually older information, glances back at what has gone before; the other announces something new. As we have seen, the older information should come first, the newer last. When it doesn't we can often just reverse the order of subjects and what follows the verb:

> *Those questions relating to the ideal system for providing instruction in home computers* are *just as confused.*

> *Just as confused* are *those questions relating to the ideal system for providing instruction in home computers.*

The switch not only puts the reference to the preceding sentences, *Just as confused* early, but it also puts at the end that information that the *next* several sentences will probably address.

> . . . instruction in home computers. For example, should the instruction be connected to some central source of information, or should . . .

Some subjects contain a relative clause full of important information that you can shift to the end of the sentence:

> A discovery *that will change the course of world history and the very foundations of our understanding of ourselves and our place in the scheme of things* is imminent.

> A discovery is imminent *that will change the course of world history and the very foundations of our understanding of ourselves and our place in the scheme of things.*

Don't shift the clause if it results in an ambiguous construction. In this next sentence, the shifted clause seems to modify *staff:*

> A marketing approach has been developed by the staff *that will provide us with a totally new way of looking at our current problems.*

3.   Extract and isolate.

If you have buried your most important idea in the middle of a very long sentence, that sentence will almost certainly swallow it up, making it considerably more difficult for you to direct your reader to the information. One way to recover the appropriate emphasis is to break the sentence in two, either just before the important idea, or if you can't do that, anywhere that's convenient, and then edit the new sentences so that you guide your reader to the information you consider crucial. That will usually mean you have to isolate the point of a long sentence by making it a single shorter sentence.

> Under the Clean Water Act, the EPA will promulgate new
> national standards for the treatment of industrial wastewater
> prior to discharge into sewers leading to publicly owned
> treatment plants, with pretreatment standards for types of
> industrial sources being discretionary, depending on local
> conditions, instead of imposing nationally uniform standards
> presently required under the Act.

First, break up the sentence:

> Under the Clean Water Act, the EPA will promulgate new
> national standards for the treatment of industrial wastewater
> prior to discharge into sewers leading to publicly owned
> treatment plants. Standards for types of industrial sources
> will be discretionary. They will depend on local conditions,
> instead of imposing nationally uniform standards presently
> required under the act.

Then rearrange in whatever ways are necessary to get the right emphasis:

> Under the Clean Water Act, the EPA will promulgate new
> national standards for the treatment of industrial wastewater
> before it is discharged into sewers leading to publicly owned
> treatment plants. Unlike the standards required under the
> present act, the new standards will not be uniform across
> the whole nation, but discretionary, depending on local con-
> ditions.

The important point here is the discretionary nature of the rules and their dependence on local conditions. It is those two ideas that the next sentence will expand on. So we express that point in its own sentence, with the point of the sentence at the end, in the stress position.

When we ignore these principles of old and new information, we write a prose that may seem both confusing and weak-sounding. Read these next few sentences aloud. Hear how your voice trails off into a lower note when at the ends of the sentences, you have to repeat words that you read earlier. Then listen to how the rewritten version lifts your voice up and then brings it down emphatically on the words that ought to be stressed.

> In 1972, the United States Supreme Court declared that com-
> ponents of a patented assembly could be produced in this
> country without infringing on US patents. Since then,
> several cases have tested whether various combinations of
> imported and domestic items could be produced without in-
> fringing on US patents. The courts have consistently held
> any combination would infringe on patents. However, the
> concept of local production and foreign assembly has not
> been tested as to infringement on patents.

Compare:

> In 1972, the United States Supreme Court declared that com-
> ponents of a patented assembly could be produced in this
> country without infringing on US patents. Since then, this
> concept has been tested by several cases involving various
> combinations of imported and domestic items. The courts
> have consistently held that US patents would be infringed by
> any combination. However, what has not been tested is the
> concept of local production and foreign assembly.

Some Syntactic Devices

There are a few grammatical patterns in English whose specific in-tention seems to be to throw special weight on the end of a sentence.

1.   There.

I wrote the sentence above without realizing that I had il-lustrated this first pattern. I could have written,

> A few grammatical patterns in English seem to have a specific in-
> tention to throw special weight on the end of a sentence.

If you begin too many sentences with *there,* your prose will become flat-footed, without movement or energy. But you can now and then begin a sentence with *there* in order to push to the end of that sentence the information on which the next few sentences will build. In other words, a *there*-sentence lets us introduce the topics for the *next* string of sentences. Again, you may remember someone telling you to avoid sentences beginning with *there.* Too many of them will measurably retard the pace of your prose. But this *there*-construction has an important function: to introduce topics that you intend to develop.

2.   What.

What a *what* sentence does is throw special emphasis on some phrase in a sentence and then add more emphasis to the end by making the reader wait a bit longer for it. I could have written,

> A *what* sentence throws special emphasis on some phrase in a sentence and then adds more emphasis to the end of the sentence by making the reader wait a bit longer for it.

Compare the emphasis of

> This country needs a monetary policy that will end the violent fluctuations in money supply, unemployment, and inflation.

> *What* this country needs is a monetary policy that will end the violent fluctuations in money supply, unemployment, and inflation.

You have to pay for added emphasis with a few more words, but if you manage this pattern judiciously, you can use the tradeoff to your benefit.

3.   *It*-shift–1.

By using *it* as an anticipatory subject, we can shift a long introductory clause to a position after the verb:

> *That domestic oil prices must eventually rise to the level set by OPEC in order to force oil conservation* once seemed inevitable.

> *It* once seemed inevitable *that domestic oil prices must eventually rise to the level set by OPEC in order to force oil conservation.*

Some editors object to this anticipatory *it* because they believe, mistakenly, that the *it* is a case of vague pronoun reference. Only in a passage with several other *its* might that be so:

> While *it* is true that *it* now requires more energy to produce
> methanol alcohol that *it* provides, *it* might well prove to be
> a cost-saving additive to fuel if *it* can be proved that *its* cost
> can be lowered substantially.

4. *It*-shift-2.

This pattern is even more obviously intended for special situations where you want very special emphasis.

Compare:

> In 1933 this country experienced a depression that almost wrecked
> our democratic system of government.

> *It* was in 1933 that this country experienced a depression that
> almost wrecked our democratic system of government.

Again, the function of the shift is to highlight a phrase and then hold off completing the sentence, thereby adding to the stress of the sentence even greater emphasis. This pattern is so obvious that you should use it sparingly.

When All Else Fails

If you find yourself stuck with a sentence that ends flatly because you have to repeat a phrase you used in a previous sentence, at least try changing the phrase to a pronoun:

> When the rate of inflation dropped in 1983, large numbers
> of investors fled the bond market and invested in *stocks*.
> However, those interested in the high tech market often did
> not carefully investigate *the stocks*.

> When the rate of inflation dropped in 1983, large numbers
> of investors fled the bond market and invested in *stocks*.
> However, those interested in the high tech market often did
> not carefully investigate *them*.

This at least throws the emphasis on the word before the pronoun, preserving the stress on a key word.

Exercise 3–1

Edit these sentences so that they end on what you would take to be their most emphatic note.

1. The catastrophic Sicilian Invasion was the most important event in Thucydides' *History of the Peloponnesian War.*
2. JD will suffer great harm if the fact that he was deprived of assistance results in his missing the deadline application.
3. There are limited opportunities for teachers to work with individual students in large American colleges and universities.
4. As used in the foundry industry, "turnkey" means responsiblity for the satisfactory performance of a piece of equipment in addition to the manufacture and installation of that equipment, according to everyone who understands the matter.
5. A gross violation of academic responsibility is required for a Board of Trustees to dismiss a tenured faculty member for cause, and an elaborate hearing procedure with a prior statement of specific charges is provided for before a tenured faculty member may be dismissed for cause.

Exercise 3–2

Edit these next sentences into more economical form, and then revise them so that they end on their strongest note. Try switching subjects and complements, changing actives and passives, shifting movable modifiers, and the like.

1. Several upper and lower eyelid reconstruction evaluation studies are presented with the aforementioned summary discussions for your general information, in addition.
2. The slow and insidious overgrowth of our basic belief system in the supremacy and importance of logical and rational processing mechanisms has to an almost complete degree sublimated mental intuition in mankind, however.
3. Overbuilding of suburban housing developments has led to the existence of extensive and widespread flooding and

economic disaster in some parts of our country in recent years, it now seems clear.

4. The teacher who makes an assignment of a long final term paper at the end of the semester and who then gives only a grade at the end and nothing else such as a critical comment is a common complaint among people who take college courses.

5. Engine fuel lines and steam heating systems in the older-type coaches also have been known to become choked with frozen ice under these particular conditions.

6. Renting textbooks for basic required courses—such as mathematics, foreign languages, and English—whose textbooks do not experience change from year to year is possible and feasible, however.

7. The course of the war and the future of world history would be changed as a result of an event that occurred at about this same point in time.

8. The effective and economical disposal of product materials that are not such that they are found to undergo biodegradation in the environment ecological system is a matter of a different nature we believe.

9. The focusing of attention on community issues that are real rather than the creation of a conversational environment which results in exhaustion in the discussion and definition of broad problem areas is of most usefulness, in the initiation of dialogue.

10. Guidelines set forth in the MLA style sheet and the NCTE guidelines for the nonsexist use of language should be adhered to by writers of papers, moreover.

11. With the fastest growing population in the region, DuPage County covers 338 square miles of land area beginning about 16 miles west of the Chicago loop.

12. An attorney who will feel a certain responsiveness to your needs and interests and who has the capability for translating your organizational problems into the most suitable legal form is your first step, it is clear.

Exercise 3-3

Revise these longer passages so that the cumulative emphasis is in the right place. You will have to take into consideration the principles of both this lesson and Lesson Four.

1. The story of King Lear and his three daughters was a popular one during the reign of Queen Elizabeth. At least a dozen easily available books offered the story to anyone wishing to read it, by the time Elizabeth died. The characters were undeveloped in most of these stories, however, making the story a simple narrative that explicitly stated rather obvious morals. When he began work on *Lear,* one of his greatest tragedies, Shakespeare must have had several versions of this story readily available to him. He turned the characters into credible human beings with complex motives, however, even though they were based on the stock figures of the legend.

2. The catastrophic Sicilian Invasion is the most important event in Thucydides' *History of the Peloponnesian War.* Three-quarters of the history is devoted to setting up the invasion of Sicily because of this. Through the step-by-step decline in Athenian society that Thucydides describes we can see how Thucydides chose to anticipate the Sicilian Invasion. What need was there to anticipate the invasion? The inevitability that we associate with the Greek tragic drama is the basic reason he did so.

3. This next passage may seem especially difficult, because it deals with content quite foreign to your knowledge. That doesn't matter. Do the revision along the lines we have been describing. Even if you believe you still do not understand the passage, you will be able to recognize whether you have made it more comprehensible.

    > Mucosal and vascular permeability altered by a toxin elaborated by the vibrio is one current hypothesis to explain this kind of severe condition. Changes in small capillaries located near the basal surface of the epithelial cells, and the appearance of numerous micro-vesicles in the cytoplasm of the mucosal cells is evidence in favor of this hypothesis. Hydrodynamic transport of fluid into the interstitial tissue and then through the mucosa into the lumen of the gut is believed to depend on altered capillary permeability.

CONTROLLING THE NUANCES OF EMPHASIS

Compare these two passages. One of them was written by W. Averell Harriman for an article in the *New York Times,* January 1, 1984.

> The Administration has blurred the issue of verification—so central to arms control. Irresponsible charges, innuendo and leaks have submerged serious problems with Soviet compliance. The objective, instead, should be not to exploit these concerns in order to further poison our relations, repudiate existing agreements, or, worse still, terminate arms control altogether, but to clarify questionable Soviet behavior and insist on compliance.

> The issue of verification—so central to arms control—has been blurred by the Administration. Serious problems with Soviet compliance have been submerged in irresponsible charges, innuendo and leaks. The objective, instead, should be to clarify questionable Soviet behavior and insist on compliance—not to exploit these concerns in order to further poison our relations, repudiate existing agreements, or, worse still, terminate arms control altogether.

In the original article, Harriman was criticizing the Republican administration on the first day of 1984, attacking what he believed were the President's misguided policies. Look at the way the two versions end, at what the stresses in each emphasize. As you probably guessed, Harriman's version is the second one, the one that stresses *blurred by the Administration, irresponsible charges, innuendo and leaks, poison our relations . . . terminate arms control altogether.* It is this second version in which Harriman comes down hard not on references to the Soviet Union, but on references to the administration.

Of course, it is precisely this ability to control emphasis that also lets us *soften* impact, hedge our emphasis. Compare the effect of these two passages:

> At the outset, this penalty might not appear to be particularly onerous. However, we are troubled by the "six months in county jail" rather than the $500 fine. The fact that the violations are criminal in nature concerns us, even though Abco has so far not received any jail sentences. It is ap-

propriate that on the basis of these dangers, the way these alleged violations are dealt with be re-evaluated.

At the outset, you might not feel that this penalty is particularly onerous. We are troubled, however, not by the $500 fine but by the "six months in county jail." Even though no Abco executive officer has received a jail sentence so far, we are concerned that the violations are criminal in nature. These dangers make it appropriate that you re-evaluate the way you deal with these violations.

The first version was in fact written by a very junior person in a corporation writing to a very senior person, someone who could indeed spend "six months in county jail"—and did not want to hear about it. And so that junior person was understandably uneasy about coming on hard with his superior. The second version is more specific, less passive, etc. But just as importantly, it also extracts the business about jail and criminal violations from the middle of the sentences and puts it at the end, where the sentences can hammer home some nasty truths. This second version sounds more confident, more emphatic.

My point here is not that being mealy-mouthed is good, but that just as we can achieve fine nuances of topic and seeming agency by controlling how we begin sentences, so can we achieve fine nuances of emphasis by controlling how we end them.

SUMMING UP
The Combined Principles of Cohesion and Emphasis

1. Cohesion

    a. Within paragraphs, try to make your topics a coherent sequence of ideas. Don't hesitate to repeat the same subject through a series of consecutive sentences.
    b. Put connecting words such as *therefore, thus, consequently, those, another,* etc. close to the beginning of their sentences.
    c. Most importantly, put at the end of the sentence the information you intend to develop in the next sentence.

2. Emphasis

   a. Put your most important ideas at the end of your sentence, and if your sentence has several clauses, arrange the ideas inside each clause so that the most important ones come last.
   b. Don't write all long or all short sentences. If you do, you will provide too few or too many points of emphasis.

The System of Clarity

By now, we begin to appreciate the extraordinary complexity of an ordinary English sentence. A sentence is more than its subject, verb, and object. It is more than the sum of its words and parts. It is a system of systems whose parts we can fit together in very delicate ways to achieve very delicate ends—if we know how. We can match, mismatch, or metaphorically manipulate the grammatical units and their related semantic meanings:

subject	verb	object
agent	action	goal

We can match or mismatch the rhetorical units and more or less important meaning:

topic	stress
old/less important	new/more important

And we can fit these two systems together into a larger system:

topic		stress	
old/less important		new/more important	
subject	verb		object
agent	action		goal

Of course, we don't want every one of our sentences to march lockstep across the page in this rigid agency-action/old-new order. When we exercise our metaphoric imagination in the way we did with the Gettysburg Address and the Baldwin passage, we can create and control fine shades of emphasis, agency, action, and point of view.

But if for no good reason we write sentences that consistently depart from that basic pattern, if we consistently hide agency, nominalize active verbs into passive nominalizations, if we consistently end sentences on secondary information, we will find ourselves writing prose that is not just confused and unclear, but prose lacking any sense of cohesion, coherence, or emphasis.

In fact, when we stand back from the details of subjects, agents, passives, nominalizations, topic, and stress, when we *listen* to the prose that we create, we should hear, feel, respond to something beyond sheer clarity and coherence. As vital as those two qualities are, they are only part of what we can call *voice*.

The voice our readers hear in our sentences contributes substantially to the character we project—or more accurately, the character our readers construct out of what we give them. When readers feel they have to slog through impersonal sentences thick with nominalizations and compounded noun phrases, they infer from that experience something about the writer's character. They will construct from that voice a character we describe variously as academic, bureaucratic, impersonal, authoritarian, aloof, gassy, ponderous. When readers read sentence after sentence that begins inconsistently and ends weakly, that swallows up its crucial point, they will construct from those sentences a writer who is unfocussed, scattered, inconsistent, uncertain, timid, cautious. Once we recognize the signs out of which readers construct these voices, and we understand how to manage the architecture of English sentences, we become free to choose the voices that best suit our purposes.

The Grammar of Concision

When we consider the richness, the good sense and strict economy of English, none of the other living languages can be put beside it.

JACOB GRIMM

The love of economy is the root of all virtue.

GEORGE BERNARD SHAW

Let thy words be few.

ECCLESIASTES 5:2

Loquacity and lying are cousins.

GERMAN PROVERB

To a Snail: If "compression is the first grace of style," you have it.

MARIANNE MOORE

O nce you can use the structure of a sentence* to support your ideas, you're a long way toward cleaning up a wordy and indirect style. But some sentences enjoy all the virtues of grammatical clarity yet remain wordy and graceless. Even when you arrange their grammatical bones in all the right ways, they can still succumb to acute prolixity:

> The point I want to make here is that we can see that
> American policy in regard to foreign countries as the State
> Department in Washington and the White House have put it
> together and made it public to the world has given material
> and moral support to too many foreign factions in other
> countries that have controlled power and have then had to
> give up the power to other factions that have defeated them.

That is,

> Our foreign policy has backed too many losers.

In the longer version, the writer matches agents* and actions* to subjects* and verbs*. But he lets his meaning ooze through too many words. He uses ten where one would have served.

To write clearly, we have to know not only how to manage the flow of our ideas but also how to express them concisely. The two principles to keep in mind are easier to state than to follow:

1. Usually, compress what you mean into the fewest words.
2. Don't state what your reader can easily infer.

We inflate our prose in so many ways that it's no use trying to list them all. But you might find it helpful to know the most common kinds of wordiness. This sentence illustrates most of them:

> In my personal opinion, we should basically listen to and think
> over in a punctilious manner each and every suggestion that is
> offered to us.

First, opinions can only be personal, so we can cut *personal.* And since the whole statement is implicitly opinion, we can cut *in my opinion. Basically* means nothing in this sentence, so we cut that too. *Listen to and think over* means *consider,* and *in a punctilious manner* means *punctiliously,* which means no more than *carefully. Each and every* is a redundant pair; we need only *each.* A suggestion is by definition something offered, and offered to someone, so neither do we need *that is offered to us.* What's left is a much leaner,

> We should consider each suggestion carefully.

SOME SIMPLE SOURCES OF WORDINESS

In these cases, you can just cross out useless words that don't add anything. You don't have to rewrite at all.

Redundant Pairs

English has a long tradition of doubled words, a habit that we acquired shortly after we began to borrow from Latin and French the thousands of words that we have since incorporated into English. Because the borrowed word usually sounded a bit more learned than the familiar native one, early writers would use both. Among the common pairs that survive are *full and complete, true and accurate, hopes and desires, willing and able, hope and trust, each and every, first and foremost, any and all, various and sundry, basic and fundamental, questions and problems,* and, *and so on and so forth.*

Redundant Modifiers

Every word implies another word. *Finish* implies *complete,* so *completely finish* is redundant. *Memories* imply *past,* so *past memories* is redundant. *Different* implies *various,* so *various different* is redundant. *Each* implies *individual,* so *each individual* is redundant. Other examples are such common phrases as *basic fundamentals, true facts, important essentials, future plans, personal beliefs, consensus of opinion, sudden crisis, terrible tragedy, end result, final outcome, initial preparation, free gift.*

In every case, we simply prune the redundant modifier. Compare:

> We should not try to anticipate *in advance* those great events that will *completely* revolutionize our society because *past* history tells us that it has been the *ultimate* outcome of little events that has *unexpectedly* surprised us.

> We should not try to anticipate those great events that will revolutionize our society because history tells us that it has been the effect of little events that has most surprised us.

Redundant Categories

Specific words imply their general categories, so we usually don't have to state both. We know that time is a period, that the mucous membrane is an area, that pink is a color, and that shiny is an appearance. So we don't have to write,

> During that *period of time,* the *mucous membrane area* became *pink in color* and *shiny in appearance.*

but only,

> During that *time,* the *mucous membrane* became *pink* and *shiny.*

In some cases, we can eliminate a general category by changing an adjective* into an adverb*:

> The holes must be aligned in an *accurate manner.*

> The holes must be *accurately* aligned.

And in some cases, we can change an adjective into a noun* and drop the redundant noun:

> The *educational process* and *athletic activities* are the responsibility of *county governmental systems.*

> *Education* and *athletics* are the responsibility of *county governments.*

In each case we can delete the general noun and leave the specific word.

Here are some common general nouns used redundantly. In every case, if we can cut the general word, we will be more direct and concise:

large in **size,** of a bright **color,** heavy in **weight,** round in **shape,** at an early **time.**

odd in **appearance,** of a cheap **quality,** honest **in character,** of an uncertain **condition,** in a confused **state,** unusual in **nature,** extreme in **degree,** of a strange **type.**

curative **process,** regulation **system,** economics **field, area** of mathematics, criminal **problem.**

Meaningless Modifiers

Some modifiers are verbal tics that we use almost as unconsciously as we clear our throats—words and phrases such as *kind of, really, basically, definitely, practically, actually, virtually, generally, certain, particular, individual, given, various, different, specific, for all intents and purposes.*

For all intents and purposes, American industrial productivity *generally* depends on *certain* factors that are *really* more psychological *in kind* than of any *given* technological aspect.

When we prune both the empty nouns and meaningless modifiers, we have a clearer and sharper

American industrial productivity depends more on psychology than on technology.

Pompous Diction

Replacing unnecessarily big words with more common ones won't necessarily cut down on the number of words you use, but it will make your diction seem sharper, more direct.

Pursuant to the recent memorandum issued August 9, 1979, because of financial exigencies, it is incumbent upon us all to endeavor to make maximal utilization of telephonic communication in lieu of personal visitation.

All of that means only,

> As the memo of August 9 said, to save the company money, use the telephone as much as you can instead of making personal visits.

There is a common word for almost every fancy borrowed one. When we pick the ordinary word we rarely lose anything important.

Sometimes, of course, the more obscure, more formal word is exactly the right one:

> We tried to negotiate in good faith but the union remains utterly intransigent.

Intransigent is not synonymous with *stubborn* or *firm* or *fixed* or *unyielding* or *uncompromising*. It means to adopt an *unreasonably* fixed position. We can, for example, be uncompromising about our moral behavior, but we would not want to say that we were *intransigent* about it, for that would suggest that we *should* compromise. So if we mean intransigent, then we should use *intransigent.*

More often, though, we choose the big word not for its precision but for its learned weight. Thus the sportscaster who intones,

> His pugilistic exploits supersede even the zenith attained by that memorable and unforgettable nonpareil of athletic endeavor, Sugar Ray Robinson.

or the police officer who reports,

> The alleged felon effectuated entrance into the domicile by means of an appliance forcibly applied to the external locking mechanism.

In a formal situation, most of us choose excessively formal language to compensate for our linguistic insecurity. We can deplore the choice and urge the writer to find simpler words. But we ought to think twice before we ridicule him. It's a natural impulse that, given the right circumstances, any of us will yield to.

A smattering of big words and their more common near-synonyms:

Contingent upon—dependent on
Endeavor—try
Utilization—use
Termination—end
Initiate—begin
Is desirous of—wants
Cognizant of—aware of
Ascertain—find out
Facilitate—help
Implement—start, create, carry out, begin

Deem—think
Envisage—think, regard, see
Avert to—mention
Apprise—inform
Eventuate—happen
Transpire—happen
Render—make, give, give back
Transmit—send
Prior to—before
Subsequent to—after

Exercise 4–1

Prune the redundancy from these sentences.

1. These various agencies and offices that provide aid and assistance services to persons who participate in our program activities have reversed themselves back from the policy that they recently announced to return to the original policy that they followed earlier.
2. It is necessary that all critics cannot avoid employing complex and abstract terms in order for them to successfully analyze literary texts and discuss them in a basically meaningful way.
3. Scientific endeavor in general depends on true and fully accurate data if it is to offer theories that will allow mankind to advance forward into the future in a safe and cautious way.
4. It is true that in spite of the fact that the educational environment is a very significant and important facet to each and every one of our children in terms of his of her own individual future development and growth, different groups and people do not all support certain tax assessments at a reasonable and fair rate that are required for the purpose of providing an educational context at a decent level of quality.

5. Most likely, a majority of all the patients who appear at the public medical clinic facility do not expect specialized medical attention and treatment because their health problems and concerns often seem not to be of a major nature and can for the most part usually be adequately treated with enough proper understanding and attention.

SOME COMPLEX KINDS OF WORDINESS

In these next cases, you have to think about your prose a bit more carefully and then rewrite a bit more extensively.

Belaboring the Obvious

Often, we are more diffusely redundant, needlessly stating what everyone knows.

> Imagine a mental picture of someone engaged in the intellectual activity of trying to learn what the rules are for how to play the game of chess.

Imagine implies a mental picture; *trying to learn* implies being engaged in the activity of; we know chess is intellectual; *chess* is a game, and games are played. The less redundant version:

> Imagine someone trying to learn the rules of chess.

Or consider this:

> When you write down your ideas, keep in mind that the audience that reads what you have to say will infer from your writing style something about your character.

You can write down only ideas; your audience can read only what you have to say; you write only to them; they can infer something about your character only from your writing style. So in fewer words,

> Keep in mind that your readers will infer from your style something about your character.

This kind of redundancy often extends through several sentences, each sentence repeating or implying what has already been stated:

> Today, the period in history known as the Holocaust is alive in the interest of many people. Dozens of films have been made, books written, and TV shows produced recording the events that took place during the Holocaust, describing the various aspects of Naziism and the systematic destruction of six million Jews by the Germans under their leader, Adolf Hitler. On the surface, this popular interest in what happened to the Jews under Hitler would appear to be a healthy phenomenon. What could be wrong with a new examination by the media of what is certainly the one single most significant event of twentieth-century history? Unfortunately, this popular interest by so many in the events of the Holocaust has brought with it serious misunderstandings about it, and inevitably incorrect views by those who have been exposed to those misunderstandings.

If we assume that what we say in one sentence doesn't always have to appear in the next, we can make this a good deal leaner and more vigorous:

> Many people have recently become intensely interested in the Holocaust through the dozens of films, books, and TV programs that have dealt with Hitler, Naziism, and the German's systematic destruction of six million Jews. On the surface, this interest would appear to be healthy: What could be wrong with reexamining the most significant event of the twentieth century? Unfortunately, this interest has also resulted in some serious misunderstandings.

Excessive Detail

Other kinds of redundancy are more difficult to prune. Sometimes, we provide too many irrelevant details.

> Baseball, one of our oldest and most popular outdoor summer sports in terms of total attendance at ball parks and viewing on television, has the kind of rhythm of play on the field that alternates between the players' passively waiting

> with no action taking place between the pitches to the bat-
> ter and exploding into action when the batter hits a pitched
> ball to one of the players and he fields it.

That is,

> Baseball has a rhythm that alternates between waiting and ex-
> plosive action.

How much detail we should provide depends on how much
our readers already know. In technical writing, addressed to an in-
formed audience, we can usually assume a good deal of shared
knowledge.

> The basic type results from simple rearrangement of the
> phonemic content of polysyllabic forms so that the initial
> CV of the first stem syllable is transposed with the first CV
> of the second stem syllable.

The writer didn't bother to define *phonemic content, stem
syllable,* or *CV* because he assumed rightly, that anyone reading a
technical linguistics journal would understand those terms.

On the other hand, this definition of *phonetic transcription,*
which would never appear in a technical journal on language, is
necessary in an introductory textbook:

> In order to study language scientifically, we need some kind
> of phonetic transcription, a system to write a language so
> that visual symbols consistently represent segments of
> speech.

A Phrase for a Word

The redundancy we've described so far results when we state what
could be left implied, a problem we can edit away simply by
testing the need for every word and phrase. But another kind of
redundancy is more difficult to edit away, because to do so we
need a precise vocabulary and the wit to use it. For example,

As you carefully read what you have written to improve
your wording and catch small errors of spelling, punctuation, and so on, the thing to do before you do anything else
is to try to see where sequences of subjects and verbs could
replace the same ideas expressed in nouns rather than verbs.

In other words,

As you edit, first find nominalizations you can replace with clauses.

We have compressed several words into single words:

carefully read what you have written		
. . . and so on	=	edit
the thing to do before you do		
anything else	=	first
try to see where . . . are	=	find
sequences of subjects and verbs	=	clauses
the same ideas expressed in nouns		
rather than verbs	=	nominalizations

There are no general rules to tell you when you can compress
several words into a single word or two. I can only point out that
you often can and that you should be on the alert for opportunities
to do so—try, that is.
     You can compress many common phrases:

the reason for	
for the reason that	
due to the fact that	
owing to the fact that	
in light of the fact that	because, since, why
considering the fact that	
on the grounds that	
this is why	

It is difficult to explain *the reason for* the delay in the completion
of the investigation.
It is difficult to explain *why* . . .

In light of the fact that no profits were reported from 1967 through 1974, the stock values remained largely unchanged.
Because no profits were reported . . .

despite the fact that
regardless of the fact that   } although, even though
notwithstanding the fact that

Despite the fact that the results were checked several times, serious errors crept into the findings.
Even though the results . . .

in the event that
if it should transpire/happen that   } if
under circumstances in which

In the event that the materials arrive after the scheduled date, contact the shipping department immediately.
If the materials arrive . . .

on the occasion of
in a situation in which   } when
under circumstances in which

In a situation which a class is overenrolled, you may request that the instructor reopen the class.
When a class is overenrolled, . . .

as regards
in reference to
with regard to   } about
concerning the matter of
where _____ is concerned

I should now like to make a few observations *concerning the matter of* contingency funds.
I should now like to make a few observations *about* contingency funds.

it is crucial that
it is necessary that
there is a need/necessity for   } must, should
it is important that
it is incumbent upon
cannot be avoided

There is a need for more careful inspection of all welds.
You *must* inspect all welds more carefully.
Inspect all welds more carefully.

It is important that the proposed North-South Thruway not
displace significant numbers of residents.
The proposed North-South Thruway *must* not displace significant
numbers of residents.

is able to has the opportunity to is in a position to has the capacity for has the ability to	can

We *are in a position to* make you a firm offer for your house.
We *can* make you a firm offer for your house.

it is possible that there is a chance that it could happen that the possibility exists for	may, might, can, could

It is possible that nothing will come of these preparations.
Nothing *may* come of these preparations.

prior to in anticipation of subsequent to following on at the same time as simultaneously with	before, after, as

Prior to the expiration of the apprenticeship period, it is incumbent upon you to make application for full membership.
Before your apprenticeship expires, apply for full membership.

increase decrease	more, less/fewer; better, worse

There has been an *increase* in the number of universities offering
adult education programs.
More universities are offering adult education programs.

We have noted a *decrease* in the quality of applicants.
We have noted that applicants are *less* qualified.

Exercise 4–2

Edit these sentences into more economical form.

1. The future that lies before those engaged in studies at the graduate school level, seeking advanced degrees from institutions of higher education, in regard to prospects for desirable employment in teaching positions at best does not have a high degree of certainty.
2. Notwithstanding the fact that all legal restrictions on the use of firearms are the subject of heated debate and argument, it is necessary that the general public not stop carrying on discussion pro and con in regard to them.
3. Under those circumstances in which individuals with financial resources to invest for a profitable return anticipate the possibility that the continually rising prices of things we buy may continue at steadily increasing rates, those individuals will ordinarily put their financial resources into specific objects of artistic value and worth.
4. In the event that governors of the various states in the United States have the opportunity at some time to get together and talk over with one another the matter of economic needs and problems in their respective states, it is possible that they will find a way to overcome the major problem they have of specifying exactly how to divide up and then distribute economic resources to their different states.
5. The major matter I want to ask about at this point is the degree to which the consciousness writers have about the individuals they create in their plays puts a disguise on the social tensions of the times in which they are writing.
6. Those engaged in the profession of education and teaching have for a long period of time been interested in having a better idea about significant improvements in how different individuals learn and commit to memory information from given written textual material. The first matter of difficulty is identifying aspects of common and different features among comparable stretches of writing. The second addresses the difficult matter of assigning some kind of value to the amount of and nature of information that a reader does not forget after that person reads a passage.

TALKING TO THE READER: METADISCOURSE

Whenever we write more than a few words, we usually have to write on two levels. We write about the subject we are addressing, of course: foreign policy, falling sales, the operation of a computer system. But we also directly or indirectly tell our audience how they should take our ideas. In those last two sentences, for example, *of course, but,* and *also* serve less to inform you than to direct you. And in that last sentence, *for example* told you how to connect the sentence to the previous two.

We need a term to distinguish writing that guides the reader from writing that informs the reader. We'll call it *metadiscourse**, discourse about discoursing. We need some metadiscourse in just about everything we write. Without it, we can't announce that we're changing the subject or coming to a conclusion, that what we're asserting is or is not certain, that our ideas are important. We can't define terms or acknowledge a difficult line of thought, or even note the existence of a reader. We can't outline what we intend to say.

We use a good deal of metadiscourse in personal narratives, arguments, memoirs—any discourse in which we filter our ideas through a concern with how our reader will take them. Except for numbers to indicate sections and so on, other kinds of writing—operating instructions, technical manuals, laws, and the like—have less metadiscourse.

The problem is to recognize when metadiscourse is useful and then learn to control it. Some writers use so much metadiscourse that they bury their ideas. For example:

> The last point I would like to make here is that in regard to
> men-women relationships, it is important to keep in mind
> that the greatest changes have in all probability occurred in
> the way men and women seem to be working next to one
> another.

Only part of that sentence addresses men-women relationships:

> . . . men-women relationships . . . greatest changes
> have . . . occurred in the way men and women . . . working
> next to one another.

The rest tells readers how to understand what they are reading:

> The last point I would like to make here is that in regard
> to . . . it is important to keep in mind that . . . in all
> probability . . . seem to. . . .

Pruned of this writing about reading, the sentence becomes a good bit more direct:

> The greatest changes in men-women relationships have occurred in
> the way men and women work next to one another.

And now that we can see what this sentence really says, we can make it even more direct:

> Relationships between men and women have changed most in the
> way they work together.

In deciding how much metadiscourse to include, we can't rely on any broad generalizations. Some entirely successful writers use a good deal of metadiscourse; others equally successful, very little. More often than not, though, it can be cut. Read widely in your field with an eye to how writers you think are clear, concise, and successful use metadiscourse. Then do as they do.

Here are some of the more common types.

Hedges and Emphatics

Each profession has its own idiom of caution and confidence. None of us wants to sound like an uncertain milquetoast or a smug dogmatist. How successfully we walk the rhetorical line between seeming timidity and arrogance depends a good deal on how we manage phrases like *a good deal,* a phrase that a few words ago allowed me to pull back from the more absolute statement:

> How successfully we walk the rhetorical line between seeming
> timidity and arrogance depends on how we manage phrases like *a
> good deal.*

Hedges, or qualifications, let us sound small notes of civilized diffidence. They leave us room to backpedal and to make exceptions. An appropriate emphatic, on the other hand, lets us underscore what we really believe—or would like our reader to think we believe.

Some of the more common hedges: *usually, often, sometimes, almost, virtually, possibly, perhaps, apparently, seemingly, in some ways, to a certain extent, sort of, for the most part, for all intents and purposes, in some respects, in my opinion at least, may, might, can, could, seem, tend, try, attempt, seek, hope.* Some of us use these so often that they become less hedges than meaningless modifiers.

Some of the more common emphatics: *as everyone knows, it is generally agreed that, it is quite true that, it's clear that, it is obvious that, the fact is, as we can plainly see, literally, clearly, obviously, undoubtedly, certainly, of course, indeed, inevitably, very, invariably, always, key, central, crucial, basic, fundamental, major, cardinal, primary, principal, essential, integral.* Words and phrases like these generally mean "believe me" and not much more. Used to excess, they sound arrogant or at least defensive. Or they become a kind of distracting background static that robs a style of any clarity or precision. This is another case where a good ear will serve you better than a flat rule.

Sequencers and Topicalizers

Sequencers and topicalizers are words that lead your reader through your text. The least useful kind of sequencers are overelaborate introductions:

> In this next section of this report, it is my intention to deal
> with the problem of noise pollution. The first thing I want
> to say about this subject is this: Noise pollution is . . .

You can usually announce the topic of a whole discourse—or any of its parts—and hint at the structure of its argument much more simply:

> The next problem is noise pollution. It . . .

Unless your paper is so complex that you have to lay out its plan in an elaborate introduction, assume that just naming the problem is sufficient to announce it as your topic, and that naming its parts suggests your organization.

Specific topicalizers focus attention on a particular phrase as the main topic of a sentence, paragraph, or whole section:

> In regard to a *vigorous style,* the most important characteristic is a short, concrete subject followed by a forceful verb.
> Sor far as the *industrial development of China* is concerned, it will be years before it becomes competitive with Japan's.
> As to the matter of *responsibility for security,* that is the problem of the buildings and grounds staff.

We use phrases and clauses such as *in regard to, where X is concerned, in the matter of, as for, as to, speaking of, turning now to,* and so on to announce that we are moving on to a new idea. But consider whether you can maneuver that new idea into the body of the sentence.

> *The most important characteristic of a vigorous style* is a short, concrete subject followed by a forceful verb.
> It will be years before China's *industrialization* becomes competitive with Japan's.
> *Responsibility for security* belongs to the buildings and grounds staff.

Probably the most common way we announce prospective topics is with *there is/are.*

> There are three reasons why we should recognize Outer Mongolia.

There is/are often occurs at the beginning of a section, announcing in the phrase that follows *is/are* the topic of that section. But whatever follows *there is/are* is always a noun phrase*, always static. So use this construction only when that phrase is important enough to develop in the next few sentences. Too many *there* *is/are*s simply present a series of topics, eventually retarding the flow of a paragraph. Compare:

> *There is* no easy way to resolve this conflict between the rich and the poor nations of the earth. *There is* a need for a greater altruism than we in the northern European countries now display, if *there is* to be an equitable distribution of the world's increasingly scarce resources and energy. And unless *there is* a solution to the problem, *there will be* a worldwide explosion into economic and racial warfare.

> We shall find no easy way to resolve this conflict between the rich and the poor nations of the earth. We in the northern European countries will have to act more altruistically than we have if we are to distribute equitably the world's increasingly scarce resources and energy. And unless we solve this problem, the world will explode into economic and racial warfare.

Attributors and Narrators

You use attributors and narrators to tell your reader where your ideas or facts or opinions came from. Sometimes, when we are still trying to work out precisely what it is we want to say, we offer a narrative of our thinking rather than its results:

> *I was concerned with* the structural integrity of the roof supports, so *I attempted* to test the weight that the transverse beams would carry. *I have concluded* after numerous tests that the beams are sufficiently strong to carry the prescribed weight, but no more. *I think* that it is important that we notify every section that uses the facility of this finding.

If we eliminate the narrators and refocus our attention on what the reader needs to know, we can make the passage a good deal more pointed:

> We must notify every section that uses the storage facility that they must not exceed the prescribed kilogram-per-square-meter floor weight. Tests have established the struc-

tural integrity of the transverse beams. They are strong
enough to carry the prescribed weights but no more than
that.

Unless your subject matter is the *way* you arrived at your observations or conclusion, you can usually be more concise and direct if you simply present the most salient observations and conclusions, minus the metadiscourse or narrative.

Some writers slip anonymous attribution into their prose more indirectly, by stating that something has been *observed* to exist, is *found* to exist, is *seen, noticed, noted, remarked,* etc.

High divorce rates *have been observed to occur* in parts of the
Northeast that *have been determined to have* especially low
population densities.
Regular patterns of drought and precipitation *have been found to
coincide* with cycles of sunspot activity.

Unless you have some good reason to hedge a bit, leave out the fact that any unspecified observor has *observed, found, noticed,* or *seen* something. Just state that it is:

High divorce rates *occur* in parts of the Northeast that *have*
especially low population densities.
Regular patterns of drought and precipitation *coincide* with cycles
of sunspot activity.

If this seems too flat-footed, drop in a hedge: . . . *apparently coincide.*

Exercise 4–3

In these next sentences, edit for both unnecessary metadiscourse and redundancy.

1. But on the other hand, however, in opposition to this, we can point out that it appears that there is going to continue to be TV programming that will on the whole appeal to what can only be considered our most prurient and, therefore, lowest interests.

2. A definition of the term *seborrhea* may be formulated in the following general way: By *seborrhea* we basically refer to an accumulation and buildup on the surface area of the skin of what would be diagnosed as abnormal or unusual sebacious secreted matter, with creation of scab formations or encrustations.

3. It may possibly turn out to be the case that the playwright known to us by the name of William Shakespeare could be someone else; perhaps someone whom we would find to be a member of royalty.

4. In this particular section, I intend to discuss my feelings about the need not to continue with the old approach to plea bargaining. I believe this is the case because of two basic reasons. The first reason that it is necessary to deal with plea bargaining is that it appears to let hardened criminals not receive their just punishment. The second reason is the following: Plea bargaining virtually always encourages a growing lack of respect for the judicial system.

5. In conclusion, I would like to point out that in regard to China, it appears to be a good example of a country on the verge of what many observers agree is going to be what could only be called a major industrial expansion.

6. Turning now to the next question to be discussed, there are in regard to the subject of wild area preservation activities three basic principles when attempting to formulate a way of approaching decisions as to those wild and uninhabited areas unspoiled by human activity that should be set aside and preserved and not developed for commercial exploitation or business enterprises.

7. It is my underlying belief that in regard to terrestial-type snakes, the assumption can be made that there are in all probability none to speak of in those unmapped areas of the world not yet explored that would be in excess of the size of those we already have knowledge of.

8. As far as I am concerned, I think that in light of the fact that Leon Trotsky was clearly and distinctly in favor of the Communist Revolution and overthrow of the Tsar, there is no possibility of arguing that he would ever have an objective viewpoint in regard to those events.

9. It seems to me that Imagism appears to mimic the haiku's use of strong visual patterns to provoke feelings and emotions at the same time that it does not accept the idea that any particular image and emotion require what we would take to be traditional correspondence.
10. As we can see, I think that in regard to the current interest in life stages, it would appear that most investigators into the area have a tendency to take the position that the midlife crisis is the most critical period or stage in a person's life development from mental health point of view; that is to say, we are in a position to know that, for the most part, a large number of us seem to come to the decision at that particular time in our lives whether or not we are going to be on the winning or losing side of the game of life.

NOT THE NEGATIVE

For all practical purposes, these two sentences mean about the same thing:

> Don't write in the negative.
> Write in the affirmative.

But if we want to be more concise and direct, we should prefer:

> Write in the affirmative.

To understand many negatives, we have to translate them into affirmatives, because the negative may only imply what we should do by telling us what we shouldn't do. The affirmative *states* it directly. Compare what you just read with this:

> "Don't write in the negative" and "Write in the affirmative" *do not mean* different things. But if *we don't want* to be indirect, then we *should not prefer* "Don't write in the negative." *We don't have to translate* an affirmative statement *in order not to misunderstand* it because it *does not imply* what we should do.

We can't translate every negative sentence into an affirmative. But we can rephrase many negatives as affirmatives, and unless you

have some special reason to emphasize a *not, no,* or *never,* look for
that affirmative sentence.

Some negatives allow almost formulaic translations into affirmatives:

> *not many* ⟶ *few*
> *not the same* ⟶ *different*
> *not different* ⟶ *alike/similar*
> *did not* ⟶ *failed to*
> *does not have* ⟶ *lacks*
> *did not stay* ⟶ *left*
> *not old enough* ⟶ *too young*
> *did not remember* ⟶ *forgot*
> *did not consider* ⟶ *ignored*
> *had nothing to do with* ⟶ *avoided*
> *did not allow* ⟶ *prevented*
> *did not accept* ⟶ *rejected*
> *not clearly* ⟶ *unclearly*
> *not possible* ⟶ *impossible*
> *not able* ⟶ *unable*
> *not certain* ⟶ *uncertain*

Now certainly this advice does not apply to those sentences
that raise an issue by contradicting or denying some point that we
intend to correct (as this sentence demonstrates). One of the most
common ways we introduce a chunk of discourse is to deny, to say
"not so" to someone else's idea of the truth, or even some possible
truth. Once we deny it, we then go on to assert the truth as we see
it:

> In the last decade of the 20th century, we will not find
> within our own borders sufficient oil to meet our needs, nor
> will we find it in the world market. The only way we will
> increase our oil supply is by developing the one resource
> that we have so far ignored: massive conservation.

When you combine negatives with passives*, nominaliza-
tions*, and compounds* in sentences that are already a bit complex, your writing can become virtually opaque:

> Disengagement of the gears is not possible without locking
> mechanism release.
> Payments should not be forwarded if there has not been due
> notification of this office.

These particular negatives all involve two events, one a precondition of the other. We can almost always recast such negatives into more direct affirmatives if we change nominalizations into clauses and passives into actives.

> In order to disengage the gears, first release the locking
> mechanism.
> Before you forward any payments, notify this office.

Which you put first—the outcome or the condition—depends on what the reader already knows, or what the reader is looking for. For example, if you are trying to explain how to reach some known objective, acquire some desired object, put that first:

> Except when applicants have submitted applications without appropriate documentation, **benefits** will not be denied.

In this case, we can assume the reader is looking for benefits. Then we put that first, but in the affirmative:

> You will receive benefits if you submit appropriate documents.

Or:

> To receive benefits, submit appropriate documents.

As you can see from this example, it is especially important to avoid using negatives along with implicitly negative verbs and connecting words such as these:

> verbs: **preclude, prevent, lack, fail, doubt, reject, avoid;
> deny, refuse, exclude, contradict, prohibit, bar,** etc.
> conjunctions: **except, unless, provided however; without,
> against, lacking, absent, but for.**

One almost formulaic translation involves the words **unless, except,** and **without,** three favorite words when we want to stipulate conditions to an action. The action made conditional is often put in the negative, with the conditions that make it possible in the clause following the **unless, without,** or **except;**

> **No** provision of this agreement will be waived **unless** done in writing by either party.

The action to be conditioned is waiver. While we might want to emphasize the importance of **not** doing something, we are ordinarily more concerned about how **to** do something. So we ought to express that action in the affirmative:

> If either party wishes to waive any provision of this agreement, he must do so in writing.

The translation almost always works:

> X may not do Y unless/except/without doing Z.

> X may do Y only if X does Z.
> In order to do Y, X must do Z.

Exercise 4–4

Where appropriate, change the following to affirmatives. Do any additional editing you think useful.

1. It is not possible to reduce inflationary pressures when the federal government does not reduce its spending.
2. Sufficient research has not been directed to the problems of individuals who cannot see when there are not normal levels of light.
3. Scientists have not agreed on the question of whether the universe is open or closed, a dispute that will not be resolved until the total mass of the universe has been computed with an error of no more than 5 percent.
4. So long as taxpayers do not refuse to pay their taxes, the government will have no difficulty in paying its debts.
5. We have no alternative to developing tar sand, oil shale, and coal as sources of fuel, because we cannot make ourselves

vulnerable to foreign powers that at any moment might not continue to supply us with oil.

6. There has not been adequate carcinogen prevention established in the chemical additive area of meat production.

7. Cancerous tumor treatment is not effective if growth removal is not accomplished before tumor metastasis.

8. Not until a resolution between Catholics and Protestants in regard to papal authority supremacy is achieved will there be the beginning of a reconciliation between the two.

9. Elections in which there is no attempt at dealing with those issues which do not receive adequate attention during the time when no election campaigns are under way cannot serve the functions for which they were intended.

10. The Insured may not refuse to provide the Insurer with all relevant receipts, checks, or other evidence of costs except when such expenses do not exceed $110.

11. Do not discontinue medication unless symptoms of dizziness and nausea fail to alleviate within six hours.

12. The lack of disconfirming evidence suggests that the results are not open to dispute, unless the absence of data from other investigations is taken as a negative factor.

13. No one is precluded from participating in the cost-sharing educational programs without a full hearing into the reasons for his or her rejection.

14. Because there have been no violations of the guidelines by HHS-supported public agencies, there appears to be no reason for the rejection of their application. The conclusion that such action was a result of political pressure cannot be avoided.

Exercise 4–5

Edit the redundancy out of these sentences. Where appropriate change negatives to affirmatives.

1 . It seems to me that in a systematic look at the nature of advertising, it is not illogical to start out with a statement that will define the term. This will establish a common point of reference so that we will not be subjective in our approach to a subject matter that is not often the topic of unemotional

discussion. Unfortunately there is no single definition for the word *advertising,* making the chances for possible objectivity not likely. This indicates that the generally popular notions about advertising cannot be examined carelessly.

2.   Regardless of the fact that we do not know for certain whether or not there is any possibility of the existence of what we would think were life forms in different parts of the universe other than the one in which we exist, it seems probable that evidence that cannot be refuted that is of a basically statistical nature makes it highly unlikely that life could not be found in a large number of planetary systems around tens of thousands of stars scattered throughout the length and the breadth of the universe as we know it.

SUMMING UP
Cutting Fat

You can cut verbal fat if you get rid of the kind of abstraction we discussed in Lesson 1. But you can also make your style leaner and more direct if you clear away the more diffuse kind of wordiness we've discussed in this Lesson. Unfortunately, I can't offer any strong generalizations to equal those I suggested about making subjects coincide with agents, verbs with actions, about old information first and new information last. Diffuse wordiness is like a chronic accumulation of specks and motes that individually seem trivial but together blur what might otherwise be a clear and concise style.

Here is a list of major sources of wordiness, along with examples and revisions.

1.   *Redundant pairs*

If and when we can define and establish our final aims and goals, each and every member of our group will be ready and willing to offer aid and assistance.

If we can define our goals, every member of our group will be ready to offer assistance.

2. *Redundant modifiers*

In this world of today, official governmental red tape is seriously destroying initiative among individual business executives.
Today, government red tape is destroying initiative among business executives.

3. *Redundant categories*

In the area of educational activities, tight financial conditions are forcing school board members to cut back in nonessential areas in a drastic manner.
In education, tight finances are forcing school boards to cut back drastically on nonessentials.

4. *Meaningless modifiers*

Most students generally find some kind of summer work.
Most students find summer work.

5. *Obvious implications*

Energy used to power our industries and homes will in the years to come be increasingly expensive in terms of dollars and cents.
In the future, energy will cost more.

6. *Pompous diction*

You must endeavor to facilitate their cognizance of the deleterious result of excessive sesquipedalianism.
You have to help them realize that big words can have bad results.

7 . *Excessive detail*

A microwave oven that you might buy in any department store uses less energy that is so expensive than a conventional oven that uses gas.
Microwave ovens use less energy than conventional ovens.

8.   *A phrase for a word*

A small sail-powered craft that has turned on its side or completely over must remain buoyant enough so that it will bear the weight of those individuals who were aboard.
A small sailboat that capsizes must float well enough to support its crew.

9.   *Excessive metadiscourse*

It is almost certainly the case that, for the most part, totalitarian systems cannot allow a society to settle into what we would perceive to be stable modes of behavior or, even more crucially perhaps, stable relationships.
Totalitarian systems cannot allow a society to settle into stable behavior or stable relationships.

10.   *Indirect negatives*

There is no reason not to believe that engineering malfunctions in nuclear energy systems cannot always be anticipated.
We can assume that malfunctions in nuclear energy systems will surprise us.

You don't have to memorize these types of redundancy, or even unfailingly distinguish one from another. What is important is an eye—or an ear—for a loose phrase, for a useless modifier, for that haze of wordiness that can afflict the prose of even the best writers when they become inattentive.

Special Problems

Pedantry consists in the use of words unsuitable to the time, place, and company.

SAMUEL TAYLOR COLERIDGE

Clear writers, like fountains, do not seem so deep as they are; the turbid look the most profound.

WILLIAM SAVAGE LANDOR

F|rom time to time, some of us have to write for an audience unable to understand easily anything but the clearest and simplest language possible. Or we may have to write on a subject so complex that even a competent reader will understand it only if we make it utterly direct and explicit. Everything we have said so far applies to either case—short sentences*, short words, a minimum of clutter, a verbal rather than a nominal style.

AUDIENCE AS AGENT

When we write for readers who do not read easily or quickly, we are often giving them immediately practical advice—how to do something like operate a machine, file a form, or rent a house. Or we may be trying to inform them about significant facts that directly affect them: about jobs, employment, politics, or their health. For such readers, information that seems dissociated from their immediate experience will seem too abstract to be meaningful, too distant to be relevant. We can make it seem immediately relevant by bringing those readers into the flow of the discourse, by making *them* agents* and goals*, and *their* experiences the action.

Here, for example, is some advice on consumerism that appeared in a publication directed to a very broad audience:

> The following information should be verified in every lease
> before signing: a full description of the premises to be
> rented and its exact location; the amount, frequency, and
> dates of payments; the amounts of deposits and pre-
> payments of rents; a statement setting forth the conditions
> under which the deposit will be refunded.

That's not particularly difficult for an educated adult. And we could make it clearer yet for an audience that reads less easily if we used all the editorial tactics we've discussed so far. But to make it clear and comprehensible for an audience that may find *any* kind of writing difficult, we should rewrite from the point of view of that audience:

> When *you* get the lease from the landlord, don't sign it right away.
> Before *you* sign, look for these things:
>
> 1. Does the lease describe the place that *you* are renting?
>
> 2. Does the lease tell *you* exactly where that place is?

3. Does the lease tell *you* how much rent money *you* have to pay? Does it tell *you* how often *you* have to pay it? Does it tell *you* on what day *you* have to pay it?

4. Does the lease say how much deposit money *you* have to give the landlord before *you* move in? Does it say how much rent *you* have to give him before *you* move in?

5. Does the lease tell *you* when the landlord can keep *your* deposit money and not give it back to *you?*

We've done more than shorten sentences, use simple words, and put agents into subjects*, and actions into verbs*. Just as important, we've made the reader's experience part of the discourse. (We've also used a tabular order with lots of white space. Had it been longer, we could have broken it up with headings and subheadings.)

While our revision is more accessible than the original, it's also longer. But we ought not assume that it's less economical—at least not if we judge economy by a measure more sophisticated than mere number of words. The real measure of economy should be whether we have achieved our ends, whether our readers understand what we want them to do and then do it.

Here is another example that might make the point clearer. It's an excerpt from an actual set of regulations intended to tell train crews how to keep one train from running into another:

When a train is moving on a main track at less than one-half the maximum authorized timetable speed for any train at that location, under circumstances in which it may be overtaken, a crew member must put off single burning fusees at rear of train at intervals that do not exceed the burning time of the fusee.

When a train is moving on a main track at or more than one-half the maximum authorized timetable speed for any train at that location, under circumstances in which it may be overtaken, crew members responsible for providing protection must consider grade, track curvature, weather conditions, sight distance, and speed of the train relative to following trains, when deciding if burning fusees should be put off.

Those two sentences have only three passives*, five harmless nominalizations*, and relatively little clutter. But at fifty-seven

and sixty-six words, they are too long, and too packed with information to be clear to a trainman who may never have gone beyond
the ninth grade. Indeed, they are a bit much for any reader.

This would be clearer:

> When you are responsible for your train, and you think another
> train might overtake you, you must put off burning fusees from
> the rear of your train. Follow these guidelines:
>
> *Condition:* Your train is on a main track, and it is moving at *less*
> than half the speed that the timetable allows for any train at that
> location.
>
> —You must put off single burning fusees often enough so that the
> second is in place before the first one burns out, and so on.
>
> *Condition:* Your train is on a main track, and it is moving at
> *more* than half the speed that the timetable allows for any train
> at that location.
>
> —You must consider these conditions when you put off fusees.
> —grade
> —sight distance
> —track curvature
> —weather conditions
> —speed of your train compared to the speed
>   of a following train

I've broken two long sentences into shorter, more comprehensible ones. I've laid the directions out in more space. I've
also used a few more words—fourteen. Does that make this version less economical? Not if we balance the cost of the paper
against the cost of a couple of trains. Short-term savings don't
always mean long-run economy. (In fact, anyone can read the
longer version faster than the shorter one as well as understand it
better.)

We can often recast even the most abstract discourse in this
way. Here is an excerpt from an article by Talcott Parsons, a social
scientist who was notorious for this opaque style:

> Apart from theoretical conceptualization there would appear
> to be no method of selecting among the indefinite number
> of varying kinds of factual observation which can be made
> about a concrete phenomenon or field so that the various
> descriptive statements about it articulate into a coherent

whole, which constitutes an "adequate," a "determinate" description. Adequacy in description is secured in so far as determinate and verifiable answers can be given to all the scientifically important questions involved. What questions are important is largely determined by the logical structure of the generalized conceptual scheme which, implicitly or explicitly, is employed.

If we edit this passage in all the ways we've discussed so far and recast it from the point of view of the reader, we can make it more accessible, at least to a moderately well-educated audience:

If you don't have a theory, you don't have a way to select from among all the things you could say about something just those things that would fit into a coherent whole, a whole that would be "adequate" or "determinate." You describe something "adequately" only when you can verify your answers to questions that scientists think are important. And they decide what questions are important on the basis of the theories that they implicitly or explicitly use.

And even that could be made more direct:

To describe something so that it fits into a coherent whole, you need a theory. When you ask a question, you need a theory to verify your answers. Your theory even determines the question you ask.

All of Parsons's qualifications don't appear in the simplest version. On the other hand, the excruciating syntax in Parsons's original must obscure those nuances from all but the most masochistically dedicated reader.

I am not suggesting that the style we're describing here is the sine qua non of good writing. In Lesson Eight we'll discuss some reasons for choosing artful complexity over utter directness. But large numbers of adults are less than entirely competent readers: By one estimate, one out of every five American adults is functionally illiterate. If so, then another must be borderline. That fact should disconcert a society increasingly dependent on information. We can agree to deplore the need to write in a manner so condescendingly simple. But if we translate our regret into a principled refusal to write in a way that may seem to some unacceptably simple, we risk letting one train slam into another.

Exercise 5–1

Rewrite these passages according to the directions.

1. This is an excerpt from an actual recall letter sent to an automobile owner. Rewrite it so that anyone who received the letter could understand just what made the recall necessary. Locate crucial actions. Use **we** and **you** as subjects of verbs expressing those actions.

> A defect which involves the possible failure of a frame support plate may exist on your vehicle. This plate (front suspension pivot bar support plate) connects a portion of the front suspension to the vehicle frame, and its failure could affect vehicle directional control, particularly during heavy brake application. In addition, your vehicle may also require adjustment service to the hood secondary catch system. The secondary catch may be misaligned so that the hood may not be adequately restrained to prevent hood fly-up in the event the primary latch is inadvertently left unengaged. Sudden hood fly-up beyond the secondary catch while driving could impair driver visibility. In certain circumstances, occurrence of either of the above conditions could result in vehicle crash without prior warning.

2. This is from Section 3102 of the Internal Revenue Code. It has to do with paying Social Security taxes for employees. Rewrite the passage so that someone who had hired a baby-sitter a few days a week would understand the provision and comply with the law rather than fire the baby-sitter out of sheer frustration.

> The tax imposed by section 3101 shall be collected by the employer of the taxpayer, by deducting the amount of the tax from the wages as and when paid. An employer who in any calendar quarter pays to an employee cash remuneration to which paragraph (7) (B) or (C) or (10) of section 3121 (a) is applicable may deduct an amount equivalent to such tax from any such payment of remuneration, even though at the time of payment the total amount of such remuneration paid to the employee by the employer in the calendar quarter is less than $50; and an employer who in any calendar year pays to an employee cash remuneration which paragraph (8) (B) of section 3121(a) is applicable may deduct an amount

equivalent to such tax from any such payment of remuneration, even though at the time of payment the total amount of such remuneration paid to the employee by the employer in the calendar year is less than $150 and the employee has not performed agricultural labor for the employer on 20 days or more in the calendar year for cash remuneration computed on a time basis.

3.   Here are excerpts from two insurance policies. Rewrite both so that anyone who can read can understand them. The first step is to break the sentences into shorter grammatical sentences.

(a)   The words "damages because of bodily injury by accident or disease including death at any time resulting therefrom" includes damages for care and loss of services and damages due to insurer liability by reason of suits or claims brought against the insured by others for the recovery of damages obtained from such others because of such bodily injury sustained by employees of the insured arising out of and in the course of their employment.

(b)   If the Insured Person, while insured under this Policy, experiences whole and continuous disability by reason of accidental injury or by reason of sickness, and is thereby prevented on account of such disability from the performance of each and every duty of his occupation, and each and every duty of all other occupations and business for remuneration or profit, for a period of more than thirty consecutive days, the Company will pay to the Policyholder or the Bank, as irrevocable creditor-beneficiary, for each day in such period on which such person remains so disabled, commencing with the thirty-first day of such period, a Daily Benefit determined in accordance with the provision entitled "Amount of Benefit" contained herein; provided, however, that the liability of the Company under the Disability Benefit is limited to payment of such benefits for a period of not more than eighteen months in connection with any one period of continuous disability. If the Insured Person suffers a recurrent disability arising out of the same cause or causes of a previous disability before the expiration of six consecutive months after the date of termination of such previous period of disability, the liability of the Company in connection with such subsequent period of disability shall be limited to the remaining portion of said eighteen-month period of benefits not exhausted during such prior period or periods of disability.

SPECIFIC AND CONCRETE

Regardless of our audience, we can make writing readable and memorable by squeezing long, windy phrases into more compact ones.

Compare:

As the number of people in our population between the ages of about eighteen to twenty-two who successfully complete their high-school education becomes smaller, institutions of higher education supported by private funds will experience increasing difficulties in maintaining the number of students enrolled at a level that will result in the continuing high quality of higher education.

As high-school graduates become fewer, private colleges will find it more difficult to keep their enrollments high enough to offer quality education.

We can also be more concrete—and therefore more memorable—if we replace general words with words that are more specific. Words come in sets. Some constitute a set of equally general things:

poodle   collie   beagle   setter

Others constitute a set that ranges from very specific to very general:

Tiki   Samoyed   dog   canine   animal   creature

Each more general member includes all those that precede it. *Tiki,* for me, unambiguously names a single entity. *Samoyed* can name Tiki, along with hundreds of thousands of other dogs. *Canine* includes all the dogs, wolves, coyotes, and dingos of the world; *animal,* all of those plus millions more; and *creature,* more yet.

To be very specific, we sometimes need more, not fewer words:

> Officials were unable to account for money spent.
> George Smith and William Winston, president and comptroller of Amtex Industries, could not explain what happened to $452,983 of company funds.

> Students who choose to major in a science here must be mathematically competent.
> Sophomores who choose to major in physics, chemistry, or geology at Southwestern U. must demonstrate that they can do calculus through differential equations.

> There must be improvements in the characteristics of our larger motors in the near future.
> Within six months, the engineering staff must design any engine over 500 horsepower to operate not two months without servicing, but four.

The more general sentences could, of course, serve as introductory statements, as topic sentences to paragraphs. Concreteness usually becomes a problem after the topic sentence. The worst writers just go on writing at that same general level.

At some point, of course, concrete and specific language becomes superfluous detail. At what point depends on the situation. Generally, writers with little authority (the young, the inexperienced, the unreliable, the unknown) need to furnish more detailed evidence to be persuasive than those with established reputations.

One style typically uses the specific to stand for the general.

Compare:

> Our students' mental health depends on their occasionally taking a break from their studies and relaxing.

> Our students' mental health depends on their occasionally closing their Aristotle and opening a Schlitz.

Wasting fuel on unnecessary driving is a sure way to guarantee that we will not have sufficient heating oil next winter.

Driving your Cadillac two blocks to the local Burger King is a sure way to guarantee that all of us will have chattering teeth next January.

We know that *Aristotle* stands for all studies, *Schlitz* for relaxation, *driving a Cadillac two blocks,* etc. for unnecessary driving. We could have used *Descartes* and *Pabst, Lincoln* and *Kentucky Fried Chicken, be wearing three sweaters* and *February,* and still have communicated essentially the same messages.

This kind of specific diction invests a style with an energy that finally can become a bit exhausting. Just as we need an occasional short sentence—or long one—to establish a supple rhythm, so the rhythm of concrete and abstract, specific and general, needs the same variation.

Exercise 5–2

Here are some very general sentences. Rewrite them so that you communicate the same idea through specific and concrete images. For example:

Many sports heroes expect too much, a situation that ordinary fans won't support much longer.

If the Richy Allens and the Larry Birds keep demanding millions a year and interest-free loans, then the Joe Doakses are going to start turning off the TV.

1. Unsophisticated TV viewers watch superficial programs rather than those of high quality.
2. People who live in big cities on the East Coast are generally threatened by street crime.
3. These days, most movie-makers are out to scare us.
4. Rock groups are becoming more concerned with showmanship than music.
5. When there were fuel shortages, many of us took vacations closer to home.
6. Some books bore me.
7. Production-line workers are becoming more interested in nonmonetary rewards for their labor.
8. You don't get very many nutrients in most breakfast cereals.

LOGICAL ORDER

When you are giving directions for a task that requires more than one or two steps, it's particularly important to be as clear and as specific as possible. Before you begin to write, list the steps in the precise order in which they must be performed. Then group them into "islands" of steps, groups of steps that constitute a larger phase or logical stages in the process. Then do the same with the islands: Group them into still larger units. In a very complex task involving a great many steps, you may even have to group the groups again.

For example, here's a list of practical steps for checking and revising your style:

1. Find phrases that you can replace with a single word.
2. Cross out whatever interrupts subject-verb and move it before the subject.
3. Circle verbs. Revise so that the crucial actions are in verbs.
4. Put a wavy line under the last few words in every sentence. If they do not express the most significant information, find that information and put it last.
5. Cross out all metadiscourse. Reread, restoring only what you must.
6. Underline all subjects. If the sequence of subjects in a paragraph does not form a coherent group, create subjects to produce a sequence that does.
7. Make a slash after every grammatical sentence*. If most exceed thirty words, break the longest into shorter sentences; if most have fewer than fifteen words, combine some into longer ones.
8 . Put a *T* over all words that provide transitions between sentences to make sure they are among the first five or six words in their sentences.
9 . Put an *A* over the agent of each action. If most significant actions seem to lack express agents or if the agents are infrequently the subjects of the verbs that name their actions, revise the sentence to make those agents subjects. Create agents where appropriate.
10. Read each sentence, dropping every word and phrase that isn't necessary to your meaning.

11. Compare the length of your subjects and complements*, and try revising when you find subjects significantly longer than complements.
12. Look for strings of compound nouns. Rewrite any that you have invented into noun + prepositional phrase*.
13. Try turning every negative into an affirmative.
14. Put an *O* over every orienter*, and try moving it to the beginning of its sentence.

That list has no internal coherence, it is a collection of seemingly unrelated items in no logical sequence. As a first step in revising that list, put together what goes together; then order the items into a logical sequence; then write a sentence that will summarize the point and function of each stage and, if necessary, a sentence or two that summarizes series of stages. This gives you a synopsis and outline of the stages of the process, a structural overview of the whole process.

If you followed that procedure with the list of fourteen items, you would have a logical sequence that you could much more easily recall. For example:

To edit your writing, you must do the following: (1) Eliminate all wordiness. (2) Consistently match your subjects, agents, and topics; match verbs and actions; match ends of your sentences and your most significant information. (3) Move to the beginning of your sentences what belongs there. (4) Break up sentences that are too long and combine sentences that are too short.

1. *Eliminate all wordiness that does not require you to significantly recast your sentence.*

    a. Read each sentence, dropping every word and phrase that does not contribute to your meaning.
    b. Cross out all metadiscourse, and then restore only what you must.
    c. Look for sequences of words that you can replace with single words.
    d. Look for strings of compound nouns, and rewrite any you have invented into noun + prepositional phrase.
    e. Try turning every negative into an affirmative.

2. *Examine your sentences to determine how consistently you have expressed significant actions in verbs, agents and topics in subjects, and significant information in stresses.*

   a. Circle each verb. If it does not express a significant action, find the most significant action and make it a verb.

   b. Put an *A* over the agent of each action. If most significant actions seem to lack express agents, or if the agents are infrequently the subjects of verbs that name their actions, revise the sentence to make those agents subjects. Create agents where appropriate.

   c. Underline all subjects. If sequences of subjects in paragraphs do not form coherent groups, create subjects that would.

   d. Put a wavy line under the last words in every sentence. If they do not express the most significant new information, find that information, and put it last.

   e. Compare the length of subjects and complements; when you find subjects significantly longer than complements, try revising.

3. *Move to the beginning of your sentences what should go there:*

   a. Put an *O* over every orienter; try to move it to the beginning of its sentence.

   b. Put a *T* over all transitional words. If they are not among the first five or six words in their sentence, try to move them there.

   c. Cross out whatever interrupts the subject-verb, and move it before the subject.

4. *Break up sentences that are too long and combine sentences that are too short.*

   a. Make a slash mark between every grammatical sentence.

   b. If most exceed thirty words, try breaking them into shorter sentences.

   c. If most sentences are shorter than fifteen words, try combining them into longer ones.

   d. Go back and redo steps 1–4.

We now have four large chunks to hold in mind, each chunk comprising no more than five smaller chunks. The larger chunks and the smaller chunks are in a logical sequence in which each step builds on a previous step. The headings sum up the chunks, and the general heading sums up the headings of the chunks. We have a structured framework into which a reader can put the specific points.

When you are writing for those who do not read easily, always underestimate their ability to follow directions, understand the point, grab the gist of what you are trying to get across. Be more patient, use more white space than you think you will need. Here is an outline of everything we have said so far.

1. Style
   a. Put your audience into the sentences as subject-agents or as object-goals.
   b. Make their crucial actions explicit verbs.
   c. Keep your sentences relatively short, from fifteen to eighteen words.
   d. Use concrete, specific words. Use few abstract nouns.
   e. Put important information at the end of your sentences.
   f. Make the topics of your sentences consistent.
2. Form
   a. Order information in a way that reflects some "natural" order—usually chronological.
   b. Use lots of headings and lots of topic-summary sentences.

Controlling Sprawl

Too much noise deafens us; too much light dazzles us; too much distance or too much proximity impedes vision; too much length or too much brevity of discourse obscures it. . . .

BLAISE PASCAL

Then said I, Lord, how long?

ISAIAH 6:11

All length is torture. . . .

WILLIAM SHAKESPEARE,
ANTONY AND CLEOPATRA, **4.14**

Too much of a good thing is worse than none at all.

ENGLISH PROVERB

O nce you've arranged your ideas in the order you want, matched their structure to the structure of the sentence*, and squeezed out the fat, you have probably also solved the problem of formless, garrulous sentences, of disorganized sprawl. But sometimes, even when you've expressed your ideas directly and economically, you can still lose a reader if you've packed too many ideas into a single sentence.

> Now that the flower children of the '60s and '70s have
> grown up to become the industrial and service workers of
> the '80s, employers have discovered that they must learn
> how to motivate a new kind of worker, who rejects the
> values of older workers, for whom a job is a means to
> achieve status and affluence, and instead looks upon labor as
> a necessary evil that he will endure only if he receives a
> high salary, generous fringe benefits, and several weeks of
> paid vacation.

The agents* and actions* are clear enough. And there is relatively little deadwood. But the sentence is too long to be clear, and, perhaps worse, it swallows up its point. For the sake of *my* point, let's agree that the point of this sentence is that employers have to learn to motivate a new kind of worker, an idea that is simply elaborated on by the rest of the sentence.

Given what we've learned about problems of topic* and stress*, we can see that the problem with a long sentence may involve more than just garrulousness. When you add clause* after clause to a sentence, you are obscuring those signals that make discourse coherent and emphatic. A long sentence lets you signal your topic prominently only once: at the beginning. And it lets you signal emphasis prominently only once: at the end. Everything else gets sucked up into a formless muddle in the middle, including what may be the *main* point of the sentence.

Compare this:

> Now that the flower children of the '60s and '70s have
> grown up to become the industrial and service workers of
> the '80s, employers have discovered that they must learn
> how to motivate a new kind of worker. These young
> employees have rejected the values of older workers, for
> whom a job was a means to achieve status and affluence. In-
> stead, they look upon labor as a necessary evil that they will
> endure only if they receive high salaries, generous fringe
> benefits, and several weeks of paid vacation.

This passage now has a topic string that more clearly directs the reader through the passage: *the flower children, employers, These young employees, they.* And perhaps more important, the point of the passage is now emphasized by being in its own sentence, whose own stress* emphasizes the new information. Then the two succeeding sentences appropriately emphasize their most important ideas:

> . . . rejected the value of older workers
> . . . a means to achieve status and affluence.
> . . . labor as a necessary evil
> . . . high salaries, generous fringe benefits, and several weeks of
>   paid vacation.

Notice too that, if we wished, we could now move that point sentence to the end of the passage, and achieve a more dramatic effect:

> The flower children of the '60s and '70s have now grown
> up to become the industrial and service workers of the '80s.
> They reject the values of older workers, for whom a job was
> a means to achieve status and affluence, and instead look
> upon labor as a necessary evil that they will endure only if
> they receive high salaries, generous fringe benefits, and
> several weeks of paid vacations. Employers have discovered
> that they must now learn how to motivate this new kind of
> worker.

TWO KINDS OF LONG SENTENCES

We have to distinguish two kinds of long sentences; the one you're reading right now, for example, is rather long, sixty-four words to be exact, but it's long simply because I have chosen to punctuate what might have been a series of shorter sentences as one long sentence; those semicolons could have been periods—and that dash could have been one too.

I can write a different kind of sentence just as long as that but one that doesn't let me trade a comma, semicolon, or dash for a period, because it is composed of several subordinate parts, all depending on a single main clause*—a sentence such as the one you are now reading, which is also exactly sixty-four words long.

Both of those sentences are single *punctuated sentences,* strings of words that begin with a capital letter and end with a period. But the first consists of shorter sentence segments, shorter coordinated* clauses* each of which could have been punctuated as a separate sentence, as in this slightly revised version:

> We have to distinguish two kinds of long sentences. The one you're reading right now, however, is rather short, sixteen words to be exact. But it's short because I have simply chosen to punctuate what might have been one long sentence as a series of shorter ones. Those periods could have been semicolons. And that last period could have been a dash.

Traditionally, we use the term *compound sentence* * to describe punctuated sentences in which we link clause to clause with semicolons or with coordinating conjunctions* such as *and, but, yet, for, so, or,* or *nor.* More than two or three such clauses in a single punctuated sentence risks a kind of breathless tumbling of ideas:

> Language was one of the great evolutionary breakthroughs in our species, *and* it probably made possible the domination of a large food-providing area by a relatively few creatures, *and* it may even have enhanced selection for intellectual power, *but* without the equally important ability to use tools, we never would have survived, *so* it is important that we analyze our evolution in both these contexts, *and* that is what this chapter will do.

Even though that is a very long punctuated sentence, it consists of several short and simple *grammatical sentences.* A grammatical sentence is a sentence that we *cannot* break into shorter sentences with just a period, no matter how long it is. Traditionally, we call these either *simple sentences,* sentences with a single clause:

> The source of certain knowledge always puzzled Socrates.

or *complex sentences,* sentences with an independent clause and at least one subordinate clause*:

> [Although there are many great dictionaries,] the greatest dictionary of them all is the *Oxford English Dictionary.*

From neither of those example sentences can we create two smaller sentences just by repunctuating. When we break a single grammatical sentence into two punctuated sentences incorrectly (as I am about to do). We have what is called a fragment. Such as the one that began *When we break* and the one you're reading right now. Here's how those fragments should have been punctuated (again, slightly revised):

> Neither of those sentences can we break into two smaller sentences, as that comma testifies. When we break a single grammatical sentence into two punctuated sentences inappropriately, we have what is called a *fragment,* such as the one that began *When we break* but not the sentence you're reading now.

Keep this principle in mind: If a very long *punctuated* sentence is also a single *grammatical* sentence, it may be difficult to read because it gives a reader no place to pause and begin again. On the other hand, if a very long punctuated sentence consists of several short grammatical sentences, it may be simple to read, but it may also sound a bit childish.

THE BEST LENGTH

We can decide how long sentences ought to be in two ways. First, we could aim at a statistical norm for different kinds of prose. In ordinary magazine writing, for example, sentences average about twenty to twenty-two words. In more technical and academic prose, they are considerably longer. In writing aimed at a very general reading public, newspaper writing for example, sentences are shorter.

The better way to think about length is to develop an eye—or ear—for when a sentence goes on too long. In practice, a grammatical sentence usually becomes too long when a writer tacks on to one clause another that modifies it, and to that clause, yet one more:

> The function of myth is to tell a story *that* will allow an interpretation *that* speaks to some problem basic to the society of its audience *because* myth is a kind of history *that* orders the world for preliterates for *whom* abstract moral or social philosophy would be irrelevant.

That's the second kind of sprawl: not several sentences within a single punctuated sentence, but a single grammatical sentence that wanders through one tacked-on dependent, subordinate clause after another.

As a first step toward sensing when your sentences begin to sprawl, find out roughly how long they run./The easiest way to find out is to put a slash mark at every period and inside every punctuated sentence where a grammatical sentence ends;/a grammatical sentence ended there, for example, and ends here./If you know roughly how many words a line of your typed or written copy averages—usually ten to fourteen—then you can tell at a glance about how many words you average per sentence./Since that one ran about three typed lines, I guess it was about thirty-three to thirty-six words long, close enough for our purposes.

If most of your sentences run more than two-and-a-half lines, you may be plain wordy, or you may be trying to pack too much into your sentences. And as a result, you may be expecting too much of your readers.

CUTTING DOWN LONG SENTENCES

The simplest way to edit sprawling sentences, particularly long punctuated sentences with lots of *ands* or *buts,* is simply to stop them with a period and delete the unnecessary conjunctions*. Compare this with the original version on page 113.

> Language was one of the great evolutionary breakthroughs in our species: It probably made possible the domination of a large food-providing area by a relatively few creatures; it may even have enhanced selection for intellectual power. But without the equally important ability to use tools, we never would have survived. It is important that we analyze our evolution in both these contexts. That is what this chapter will do.

Because *and* usually just means "Here's one more thing,' you can usually drop *and.* You can also drop most *so*s. If you find that you can't, the flow of your argument may need some attention: Logical conclusions should be obvious from what preceded them.

Ordinarily, you can't omit a *but* or *yet.* You have to signal qualifications and contradictions. When we remove the *but,* the sentence beginning with *Without* seems disjointed:

> Language was one of the great evolutionary breakthroughs in our species: It probably made possible the domination of a large food-providing area by a relatively few creatures; it may even have enhanced selection for intellectual power. Without the equally important ability to use tools, we never would have survived. It is important that we analyze our evolution in both these contexts. That is what this chapter will do.

As a general rule, if a clause beginning with *but* or *and* introduces a major point that you intend to develop, punctuate that clause as a separate sentence:

> We must acknowledge that the United States government has a long history of broken treaties with the Indian nations *that trusted it, but it is equally true* that in recent history, it has attempted to redress many of those broken agreements. In Maine, for example, the federal government has . . .

Beginning a new sentence at *But it is equally true* makes the thesis more prominent:

> We most acknowledge that the United States government has a long history of broken treaties with the Indian nations *that trusted it. But it is equally true* that in recent history, it has attempted to redress many of those broken agreements. In Maine, for example, . . .

However, when the clauses are short and the *but*-clause is closely tied to the preceding clause, you gain little except special emphasis by splitting them with a period:

> Prices are *going up, but wages* are going up a bit faster.
> Prices are *going up. But wages* are going up a bit faster.

While long sentences containing several grammatical sentences can simply be repunctuated, splitting up long grammatical sentences takes a bit of rewriting. Here are some ways to do it.

Splitting before an *And*

If the sentence consists of long coordinate verb phrases*, stop before the *and* or *but* and find subjects* for the second verb phrases.

> Students of animal behavior *have been concerned* with the problem of the sensory control of motivation and emotion during periods of unusual stress *and have studied* the behavior of many species under controlled conditions of various kinds.

> Students of animal behavior *have been concerned* with the problem of the sensory control of motivation and emotion during periods of unusual stress. *They have studied* the behavior of many species under controlled conditions of various kinds.

Splitting before *although/because/if*

In these cases, we first have to turn a subordinate clause into an independent clause. The most convenient way to start is by breaking a long sentence just before or after a dependent clause beginning with *although, because, if* and so on. You then have to replace that *although, because, if* with a new sentence connector.

1. *although, though, while* ⟶ *but, yet, however. Although* and *but* signal qualifications in different ways. When we read a sentence that begins with *although,* we have to keep in mind that the first idea is going to be contradicted by what follows. But (as in this case) when the contradiction is signaled by *but* or *however,* you have to recall the previous sentence to qualify it.

   Although the court ordered the police to remain on the job until the injunction against the strike had been set aside by a higher court, they refused the order and went out on strike regardless of the penalties that they knew would be levied against them.

   The court ordered the police to remain on the job . . . set aside by a higher court. **But** they refused the order and went out on strike . . .

   This is one reason why you want to put *however, on the other hand,* and so on close to the beginning of their sentences. When you signal your contradiction at the end of a sentence, you force your reader to go back *two* full sentences to make sense out of the pair:

Legalized gambling is a potentially rich source of tax revenue for traditionally underfinanced areas of public administration. In most places where gambling has been legalized, it has proven to be a source of serious social problems, **however.**

If the writer had put the *however* earlier, the reader would not have to backtrack:

. . . areas of public administration. In most places where gambling has been legalized, **however,** it has proven . . .

2. *because, since,* ——▶ *as a result, consequently, for, so, because of this.* How you split cause-and-effect sentences linked with *because* or *since* is more complicated. When the *because-*clause comes first, you can start the second sentence with *as a result, consequently,* and so on. Avoid *this had the result of, this resulted in, this led to,* or *this had the effect of,* because the prepositions* at the end of those phrases will force you into awkward nominalizations*:

Because the soaring cost of energy, the most important factor in the world economy of the late twentieth century, has shaken the confidence of the world in the industrialized nations' ability to sustain a healthy rate of growth, *fewer economists predict* that the less developed nations can look forward to a reasonably promising future.

The soaring cost of energy, the most important factor in the world economy of the late twentieth century, has shaken the confidence of the world in the industrialized nations' ability to sustain a healthy rate of growth. **This has resulted in** *fewer predictions by economists* that the less developed nations can look forward to a reasonably promising future.

Compare that awkward *fewer predictions by economists* with a sentence that begins with *as a result, consequently,* or even *because of this:*

. . . ability to sustain a healthy rate of growth. **As a result,** *fewer economists predict* that the less developed nations. . . .

When you split a sentence that begins with the effect and ends with a *because*-clause (the cause), splitting up gracefully is a bit more difficult. English doesn't have an idiomatic connective parallel to *therefore* or *as a result* to signal that the second clause is a cause. Occasionally, *for* will serve:

Many of our older cities are facing fiscal crises far worse than any they have thus far experienced. **For** facilities that were built years ago are deteriorating and will have to be completely replaced in the not-too-distant future.

But *for* is weak and a bit formal, and won't do for long, complex sentences about complex causes. There are other introductions, but four of them end in prepositions that force us into muddy nominalizations. Don't begin sentences with *this was caused by/resulted from/was owing to/was due to:*

. . . crises that are far worse than any they have thus far experienced. **This is due to** *the deterioration of facilities* that were built years ago. . . .

Compare:

. . . crises that are far worse than any they have thus far experienced. **This has happened because** *facilities that were built years ago have deteriorated* and will need . . .

3. *if, provided that,* ⟶ *if so, if this happens.* Just as English lacks a graceful connecting word to signal the cause of something described in a preceding sentence, so it lacks a graceful connecting word that would signal the condition for something previously mentioned as its consequent.

Compare:

If demographic changes continue as they have over the last several years, shrinking the population by as much as 25 percent, *we may find it difficult* to go on supporting a large elderly population on the taxed earnings of a relatively small labor force.

Demographic changes could continue as they have over the last several years, shrinking the population by as much as 25 percent. **If that happens,** *we may find it difficult* to go on supporting a large elderly . . .

The implicitly negative conditionals *unless* and *except(ing) that* sometimes make for difficult reading, especially when they combine with explicit negatives:

The regulation will **no** longer govern this situation, **unless** the Agency does **not** decide to review it.

Avoid negatives in general (review pp. 88–91), but especially with conditionals. You can almost always translate a negative conditional by deleting the negative and changing the *unless* to *only if.*

No royalties will be paid under this agreement, **unless** the parties agree.

Royalties will be paid under this agreement **only if** the parties agree.

Whether we put qualifications, causes, or conditions before or after the sentences they qualify depends entirely on issues we dealt with in Lessons Two and Three. The principle is a simple one: Whatever you intend to expand on, explain, analyze—put it last, to introduce that expansion, explanation, or analysis.

Although legalized gambling can create serious social problems, it is potentially a rich source of tax revenue. Both Nevada and New Jersey have realized several millions of dollars . . .

If the writer had intended to pick up on the social problems, then the clause referring to them should appear last:

Although legalized gambling is potentially a rich source of tax revenue, it can also create serious social problems. Communities in which such gambling is allowed have experienced sharp increases in prostitution, robbery, loan sharking. . . .

Because a clause introduced by *although* almost always feels distinctly secondary to the main clause it modifies, avoid putting it after that main clause. It will sound like a tacked-on afterthought.

Legalized gambling is a potentially rich source of tax revenue, **although** it carries with it social risks that we might want to avoid.

If you feel you can't rearrange the sentence but you want to emphasize what that *although*-clause signals, change the *although* to *even though:*

Legalized gambling is a potentially rich source of tax revenue, **even though** it carries with it social risks that we might want to avoid.

Some writers believe that it is wrong to begin a sentence with a clause beginning with *since*. They believe that *since* may signal only a relationship in time. That is grammatical folklore. *Since* also signals conditions that the writer believes the reader will (or should) take for granted.

Since the Russians have regularly violated every treaty they have signed, we must insist on on-site verification of any future agreement.

We must insist on on-site verification of any future agreement with the Russians, **because** they have regularly violated every treaty they have signed.

In the first sentence, the writer takes for granted that we will agree that the Russians have violated treaties. In the second, the writer *asserts* that they have regularly violated every treaty. The difference is a subtle one, but there. The writer who wants to induce the reader to accept presupposed claims will couch those presupposed claims in subordinate clauses and either put those clauses first or bury them inside the sentence. It is a sly variation on "Have you stopped beating your wife?"

Splitting before a *which/who/that*-clause

A string of relative clauses is invariably limp and graceless. We can correct it by simply cutting the string at some appropriate place.

Of all the areas of scientific advancement that are important not just to the future of science but to everyday life on this planet, few have consequences more potentially awesome than genetic engineering **that** manipulates the elemental structures and units of life itself, **which** are the genes and chromosomes **that** direct our cells how to reproduce and become the functional parts of all life forms.

Of all the areas of scientific advancement that are important
not just to the future of science but to everyday life on this
planet, few have consequences more potentially awesome
than genetic engineering. **Genetic engineering** manipulates
the elemental structures and units of life itself. **These** are
the genes and chromosomes **that** direct our cells how to
reproduce and become the functional parts of all life forms.

When a *which* refers to the whole of the preceding clause, find a
subject that will replace the *which* and begin a new sentence.

Mapmaking in Europe entered a renaissance in both theory
and practice during the sixteenth and seventeenth centuries,
which was the result of exploration and colonization of the
New World and commercial relations with Asia.

Mapmaking in Europe entered a renaissance in both theory
and practice during the sixteenth and seventeenth centuries.
This development resulted from the exploration and colonization of the New World and from commercial relations with Asia.

Splitting with a Colon

If a sentence contains a long list, you can help the reader by introducing it with a colon. But remember that you ought to have a
complete sentence **before** the colon.

In order to analyze the structural properties of discourse, it
is necessary **to account for: the flow of semantic**
information in the paragraph, the devices used to achieve
coherence, and the functional units in paragraphs such as
topic sentences.

In order to analyze the structural properties of discourse, it
is necessary to account **for the following: the flow of**
semantic information in a paragraph, the devices. . . .

(Note: Most handbooks recommend beginning the section
after a colon with a lower-case letter. If what follows the colon is
not a complete clause, you can still begin with the lower-case let-

ter. But if you have finished one clause and are beginning another complete clause, you can signal that fact to your reader by beginning that next clause with a capital letter: This clause is an example.)

Exercise 6–1

All these sentences are too long. Split them into smaller units; then edit them in the ways we've been discussing.

1. Several activities have already evolved at this college in response to the problems identified in the self-study to meet the ever-expanding range of student learning desires, styles, and capabilities, and these new programs also relate to the traditional goals of the college, which include education of the whole person in the basic skills of liberal education.

2. Two themes that are not separated in their discussion are: first, the apprenticeship nature of graduate medical training, which is therefore at base not a formal process, and, second, teaching competence in the three areas of professional learning, including knowledge, technique, and behavioral skills and attitudes, which require that graduate medical training not exclude formal instruction and work in classroom contexts.

3. Regardless of the fact that it is true that the training program has a long financial problem history and management staff dispute record as a result of unclear organizational responsibility definition, it is equally true that in the period of the last few years or so, it has with considerable success placed in the area of 50 percent of its trainees in various different jobs and positions equal to their training and skill-level preparation.

4. Being alone and being lonely are not the same feeling that a person has resulting from how well that person can draw on resources that he or she has developed during the time he or she was growing into adulthood, which is the period in our lives when we all have to face up to who we are and whether we can live with ourselves for the rest of our lives.

5. As a result of the fact that soaring energy costs have especial-
    ly placed a burden on those who can least afford the added
    expense of the energy they use every day—the sick, the older
    people, and others whose income does not change—and who
    can least endure the difficult hardship of lower temperatures,
    we must create and implement a program of action that would
    identify those various individuals who can least afford to set
    their temperatures at a lower level and then provide subsidy
    support for their oil or gas or coal fuel supply costs.

6. Many city dwellers find it a necessity to give up on life as it
    exists in the city at the present time as a consequence of
    things such as dirt and crime that finally defeat them despite
    the fact that on the occasion of their leaving for more rural
    environs, they often come to the realization that they wish
    they again had the intensity and excitement that makes life in
    the city such a stimulating experience.

7. Nothing offers a test and a challenge of our basic belief in the
    principle of free speech in a more severe way than the Nazi
    party of America, which deliberately holds marches and
    rallies in Jewish communities to enrage those various citizens
    that experienced the most pain and suffering and misery
    from German Naziism, so that they will arouse violent reac-
    tions which will simply give them more money than before.
    tract additional members and more money than before.

8. An institution or organization that is disappearing from the
    general business life in this country is known as the men-only
    club, that seems to have traditionally provided a place where
    business deals and arrangements could be brought to a con-
    clusion in an atmosphere of an intimately male character, for
    the reason that increasing numbers of women have no reluc-
    tance about exercising a business power and might that once
    was in the possession only of men and so demand the same
    amenities and conveniences that once were the privilege of
    men alone.

9. The underlying basic assumption of this procedure presup-
    poses: a large enough sample size sufficient so that it does not
    result in the exclusion of a range of variation that we would
    not be surprised to find in the total population involved, an
    analysis not in contradiction with accepted statistical

methodological procedures, and a replication of the study under conditions which have no significant differences from those that existed in other studies of this kind.

10. Lear experiences a failure in the ability to recognize the faithlessness of Goneril and Regan and the honesty of Cordelia and the Fool and also cannot recognize who the disguised Kent is, who through a kind of flattery that is like that of Lear's faithless daughters creates in Lear the belief that he serves him, for despite the fact that Kent's intentions are of an honorable kind, his flattery of Lear as someone who would be his "master" is a kind of deceit which takes advantage of the vanity of Lear, and even gives encouragement to it.

SUMMING UP
Controlling Sprawl

Here's a checklist for controlling sprawling sentences.

1. Take a quick inventory of your sentence length. Put a slash mark at the end of every punctuated sentence. For those sentences that you immediately recognize as running more than three or so lines, check them for smaller grammatical sentences: put a slash mark between all grammatical sentences inside punctuated sentences.
2. Consider whether two or more grammatical sentences inside a single punctuated sentence might read more clearly if they were punctuated as separate sentences. Look especially carefully at shorter grammatical sentences that express an important point. Don't crowd them into a long punctuated sentence with other less important elements. Set them off as separately punctuated sentences:

    In the 1950s several researchers mapped areas of the brain by stimulating various cortical points with small electrical charges; as different parts of the brain were stimulated, subjects reported verbally the sensations they experienced, and what scientists were astonished to discover was that we can recall from deep inside our brains memories that would otherwise have remained locked away forever.

In the 1950s several researchers mapped areas of the brain by stimulating various cortical points with small electrical charges; as different parts of the brain were stimulated, subjects reported verbally the sensations they experienced. **Scientists** were astonished to discover that we can recall from deep inside our brains. . . .

3.   If a long punctuated sentence does *not* consist of shorter grammatical sentences that you can merely repunctuate, consider more extensive rewriting.

   a.   If your sentence contains two or more long, coordinate verb phrases after the subject, put a period after the first verb phrase. Then repeat the topic/subject* to change the second verb phrase into an independent sentence:

We first postulated cost-benefit curves for the change-over extending through 1987, taking into consideration the anticipated rate of inflation through that time, **and then projected** a profit ratio to determine whether the investment risk justified our allocating 75 percent of our research efforts in this area.

. . . the anticipated rate of inflation through that time. **We then projected** a profit ratio. . . .

   b.   If your sentence concludes with a long relative clause beginning with a *which* that refers to all that precedes it, replace the *which* with a *this* + noun, and begin a new sentence:

Increasing numbers of undergraduates are looking to the master's degree in business administration as their passport to financial success and a world of challenge and excitement, **which** reveals how much students have changed from the more politically and socially aware years of the '60s.

. . . challenge and excitement. **This new interest** reveals how much students have changed from. . . .

c. If your already long sentence concludes with a long relative clause, rewrite the relative clause as an independent sentence:

If those of lower socioeconomic origins decline to participate in these studies and if their economic status is related to the effectiveness of the treatments, then the study will not effectively evaluate the therapy for the nonparticipating group, **which** as a result may undergo a therapy that is not appropriate to their special medical needs.

. . . will not effectively evaluate the therapy for the nonparticipating group. **This group,** as a result, may undergo a therapy that is not appropriate. . . .

d. If your sentence has a long adverbial clause beginning with *because, although, if,* etc. delete the conjunction and introduce an appropriate sentence connector:

Although in Elizabethan England the rate of inflation was higher than it ever had been or would ever be again for another three centuries, peasants were less affected than we might expect **because** many of them grew their own food, made their own clothing, and relied less on the exchange of coin than on the exchange of kind.

In Elizabethan England the rate of inflation was higher than it ever had been or would ever be again for another three centuries. **But** peasants were less affected than we might expect: Many of them grew their own food, made their own clothing, and relied less on the exchange of coin than on the exchange of kind.

(Note that we replaced an initial *although* with a subsequent *but* and substituted a colon for a *because.)*

4. Finally, reread what you have done, to make sure that the *order* of the new sentences is appropriate. Be particularly sure that the topic-stress sequence works. Do the sentences have a consistent topic? Does the stress of one sentence lead into the next? And finally, does the central point of the originally long sentence stand out in the way you want it to? Is it worth ex-

pressing in a single short sentence? Do you want it to introduce the new string of sentences, or do you want to lead up to it?

Compare:

> Plain English laws are beginning to appear in increasing numbers of states because legislators are beginning to realize that the general public is not well served by guarantees, contracts, patient consent forms, and so on that require an advanced degree to understand, although in many states lawyers are objecting to any changes at all because they fear either litigation over any new language or the reduced fees that less litigation would bring them.

> Plain English laws are beginning to appear in increasing numbers of states. In many states, however, lawyers are objecting to any changes at all. They fear litigation over any new language. Or they fear the reduced fees that less litigation would bring them. But legislators are beginning to realize that the general public is not well served by guarantees, contracts, patient consent forms, and so on that require an advanced degree to understand.

> Legislators are finally beginning to realize that the general public is not well served by guarantees, contracts, patient consent forms, and so on that require an advanced degree to understand. In many states, it is true, lawyers are objecting to any changes at all. They fear litigation over any new language. Or they fear the reduced fees that less litigation would bring them. But Plain English laws are beginning to appear in increasing numbers of states.

Which of the rewritten versions we prefer would depend on what we want to do with this passage: Are we summing up, introducing, explaining? What impact do we want to achieve? At this point, mechanical rules must yield to judicious choice.

Managing Long Sentences

Sentences in their variety run from simplicity to complexity, a progression not necessarily reflected in length: a long sentence may be extremely simple in construction—indeed must *be simple if it is to convey its sense easily.*

SIR HERBERT READ

A long complicated sentence should force itself upon you, make you know yourself knowing it. . . .

GERTRUDE STEIN

The ability to write clear, crisp sentences* that never go beyond twenty or so words is a considerable achievement. You'll never confuse your reader with sprawl, wordiness, or muddy abstraction. But if you never write a sentence longer than twenty words, you'll be like a pianist who uses only the middle octave: You can carry the tune but not with much richness or variation.

Every competent writer has to know how to write a concise sentence and how to edit a long one down to comprehensible length. But a writer also has to know how to manage a long sentence gracefully, how to make it as clear and as vigorous as a series of short ones.

Now, several long clauses* in a single grammatical sentence* do not in themselves constitute formless sprawl. Here is a sentence with eighteen subordinate clauses, seventeen of them leading up to a single main clause* and the eighteenth bringing up the end:

> Now if nature should intermit her course and leave altogether, though it were but for a while, the observation of her òwn laws; if those principal and mother elements of the world, whereof all things in this lower world are made, should loose the qualities which now they have; if the frame of that heavenly arch erected over our heads should loosen and dissolve itself; if celestial spheres should forget their wonted motions, and by irregular volubility turn themselves any way as it might happen; if the prince of the lights of heaven, which now as a giant doth run his unwearied course, should, as it were through a languishing faintness, begin to stand and to rest himself; if the moon should wander from her beaten way, the times and seasons of the year blend themselves by disordered and confused mixture, the winds breathe out their last gasp, the clouds yield no rain, the earth be defeated of heavenly influence, the fruits of the earth pine away as children at the withered breasts of their mother no longer able to yield them relief—what would become of man himself, whom these things now do all serve?
>
> —Thomas Hooker, *Of the Laws of Ecclesiastical Polity,* 1594

Whatever else we may want to say about that sentence, it does not sprawl. Its Ciceronian intricacy no longer appeals to most modern ears, but its clauses fit together as neatly as the universe Hooker describes. So it is not length alone, or number of clauses alone, that we ought to worry about, but rather long sentences without shape or rhythm.

There are a few simple ways you can extend the line of a sentence and still be graceful and clear. The easiest is coordination*.

COORDINATION

We can join grammatically equal segments with *and, but, yet* or *or* anywhere in a sentence. But we do it most gracefully after the subject*, in the predicate*. If we create a long subject, our reader has to hold his breath until he gets to a verb*:

Public service advertising that
trumpets corporate altruism

and

commercial advertising that tries
to increase sales

⎱ sometimes serve conflicting interests.

An advertisement that urges us to
buy an outdoor barbecue fueled by
natural gas

and

another that tells us to save money
by turning down our thermostats to
68°,

⎱ for example, cannot be easily reconciled.

If these sentences had shorter subjects and longer predicates they would move along with a bit more grace:

Sometimes there is a conflict of interest between

⎰ public service advertising that
trumpets corporate altruism
and
commercial advertising that tries to
increase sales.

For example, it's difficult to reconcile
{
an advertisement that urges us to buy an outdoor barbecue fueled by natural gas
and
another that tells us to save money by turning down our thermostats to 68°
}

In general, a vigorous sentence moves quickly from a short and concrete subject through a strong verb to its complement*, where we can, if we wish, more gracefully elaborate our syntax and more fully develop our ideas. So if we extend a sentence by deliberately coordinating parts of it, we should coordinate after the subject more often than before the verb.

In using coordination to build longer sentences, we have to avoid two problems.

1. *Faulty Parallelism.* When we coordinate sentence parts that have different grammatical structures, we may create an offensive lack of parallelism. A common rule of rhetoric and grammar is that we can coordinate elements only of the same grammatical structure: clause and clause, predicate and predicate, prepositional phrase* and prepositional phrase. Most careful writers would avoid this:

These advertisements persuade us
{
that the corporation supports environmentalism
but not
to buy its frivolous products.
}

Corrected:

. . . persuade us
{
that the corporation supports environmentalism
but not
that we should buy its frivolous products.
}

This also would be considered nonparallel:

The committee recommends

{
completely revising the curriculum in applied education in order to reflect trends in local employment

and

that the administrative structure of the division be modified to reflect the new curriculum
}

Corrected:

. . . recommends

{
that the curriculum in applied education be completely revised in order to reflect trends in local employment
and
that the administrative structure of the division be modified to reflect the new curriculum.
}

And yet some nonparallel coordinations occur in well-written prose fairly often. Writers frequently join a noun* phrase with a *how*-clause:

Every attempt will be made to delineate

{
the problems of biomedical education among the underdeveloped nations

and

how a coordinated effort can address them in the most economical and expeditious way.
}

Or an adjective* or adverb* with a prepositional phrase:

The grant proposal appears to have been written

{
intelligently,
carefully,

and

with the full cooperation of all the agencies whose interests this project involves.
}

Some teachers and editors would insist on rewriting these into parallel form:

$$
\ldots \text{ to delineate}
\begin{cases}
\textit{the problems} \text{ of biomedical education} \\
\text{and} \\
\textit{the coordinated effort} \text{ necessary for the most economical and expeditious solution.}
\end{cases}
$$

$$
\begin{array}{l}
\text{The grant proposal} \\
\text{appears to have been} \\
\text{written with}
\end{array}
\begin{cases}
\textit{intelligence,} \\
\textit{care,} \\
\text{and} \\
\textit{the full cooperation of} \ldots
\end{cases}
$$

But most educated readers don't even notice the "faulty" parallelism here, much less find it offensive.

2. *Lost Connections.* What will bother readers more than mildly faulty parallelism is a grammatical coordination so long that they either lose track of its internal connections or, worse, misread those connections:

> Every teacher ought to remind himself daily that his
> students are vulnerable people, insecure and uncertain about
> those everyday, ego-bruising moments that adults no longer
> concern themselves with, and that they do not understand
> that one day they will become as confident and as secure as
> the adults that bruise them.

That momentary flicker of hesitation about where to connect

> . . . and that they do not understand that one day they . . .

is enough to interrupt the flow of the sentence.

If you can't bring the second coordinate element closer than ten or twelve words to where it begins, try repeating a key word that connects with the second coordinated member.

> Every teacher ought *to remind* himself daily that his
> students are vulnerable people, insecure and uncertain about
> those everyday, ego-bruising moments adults have learned

to cope with, *to remind himself* that his students do not
understand that one day they will become as confident and
as secure as the adults who bruise them.

And, of course, you can always begin a new sentence:

. . . adults no longer concern themselves with. Teachers should
remind themselves that their students do not understand . . .

EXTENDING THE SENTENCE

Resumptive Modifiers

A simple device that lets you extend the line of almost any
sentence we will call a *resumptive modifier**. Simply repeat a key
noun, verb, or adjective and then resume the line of thought,
elaborating on what went before. It is a pattern that lets the reader
pause for a moment, then move on.

Compare:

For several years the Columbia Broadcasting System created and
developed situation comedies that were the best that American TV
had to offer, such as "The Mary Tyler Moore Show" and "All in
the Family" that sparkled with wit and invention.

For several years, the Columbia Broadcasting System created and
developed situation **comedies** that were the best that American TV
had to offer,
          comedies such as "The Mary Tyler Moore Show"
          and "All in the Family,"
          comedies that sparkled with wit and invention.

At best, that first sentence verges on rhythmic monotony.
The writer tacked on a relative clause*, *comedies that were the
best,* and then without a pause a second, *"the Family that sparkled
with wit and invention.* The resumptive modifier in the revision
lets us pause for a moment, catch our breath, and then move on.

You can pause and resume with parts of speech other than nouns. Here with adjectives:

> It was American writers who first used a vernacular that was both **true** and **lyrical,**
> > **true** to the rhythms of the working man's speech,
> > **lyrical** in its celebration of the land.

Here with verbs:

> Man has been defined by some as the only animal that can **laugh** at grief,
> > **laugh** at the pain and tragedy that define his fate.

Summative Modifiers

Somewhat similar is the *summative modifier.* * With a summative modifier, you end a segment of a sentence with a comma, sum up in a noun or noun phrase what you have just said, and then continue with a relative clause.

Compare these:

> In the last five years, our population growth has dropped to almost zero, **which** in years to come will have profound social implications.

> In the last five years, our population growth has dropped to almost zero,
> > **a demographic event that** in years to come
> > will have profound social implications.

> Scientists have finally unraveled the mysteries of the human gene, **which** may lead to the control of such dread diseases as cancer and birth defects.

> Scientists have finally unraveled the mysteries of the human gene,
> > **a discovery that** may lead to the control of such dread diseases as cancer and birth defects.

The summative modifier avoids the gracelessness and the potential ambiguity of a vague *which* and lets the writer extend the line of the sentence without slipping into a drone.

Free Modifiers

A third kind of modifier that lets you continue the line of a sentence and still avoid monotony resembles the previous two but functions a bit differently. It follows the verb but comments on the subject. It usually makes more specific what you assert in the preceding clause.

Compare:

> However violent King Kong appeared, he always had a hint of the noble savage about him who protected his fair captive against prehistoric monsters and who treated her with the gentleness of an exceptionally hairy and overgrown but basically decent Tarzan.

> However violent King Kong appeared, he always had a hint of the noble savage about him,
>> **protecting** his fair captive against prehistoric monsters,
>> **treating** her with the gentleness of an exceptionally hairy and overgrown but basically decent Tarzan.

These free modifiers most often begin with an **-ing** participle:

> The Scopes monkey trial was a watershed in American religious thinking,
>> **legitimizing** the contemporary interpretation of the Bible and
>> **making** literal fundamentalism a backwater of anti-intellectual theology.

But they can also begin with a past participle* form of the verb:

> Leonardo da Vinci was a man of powerful intellect,
>> **driven** by an insatiable curiosity and
>> **haunted** by a vision of artistic expression.

Or with an adjective:

> In 1939 the United States began to assist the British in their struggle against Germany,
>> **fully aware** that it was involving itself in another world war.

Exercise 7–1

In these next sentences, create resumptive, summative, and free modifiers. The first five have a word in italics to use as the start of the resumptive modifier and a word in parentheses at the end to use as the start of the summative modifier. Then pick four or five sentences and create a free modifier on your own. For example:

> Within ten years, we could meet 25 percent of our energy needs with solar *energy.* (a possibility)

Resumptive:

> Within ten years, we could meet 25 percent of our energy needs with solar *energy, energy* that is safe, cheap and plentiful.

Summative:

> Within ten years, we could meet 25 percent of our energy needs with solar energy, *a possiblity* that no one could have anticipated just ten years ago.

Free:

> Within ten years, we could meet 25 percent of our energy needs with solar energy, freeing ourselves of dependence on OPEC oil.

(Many of these sentences can also be edited for redundancy, wordiness, heavy nominalizations, etc.)

1. Many different school systems are making a return back to old-fashioned traditional education in the *basics.* (a change)
2. Within the period of the next few years or so, automobile manufacturers will not be able to avoid meeting new and more stringent-type mileage *requirements.* (a challenge)
3. The reasons for why we age are a *matter* that has puzzled and perplexed humanity for millennia. (mystery)
4. The majority of the young people in the modern world of to-day cannot even begin to achieve an understanding or grasp of the *insecurity* that a large number of older people had experience of during the period known as the Great Depression. (a failure)

5. The successful accomplishment of test-tube fertilization of embryos raised many *issues* of an ethical nature that continue to trouble both scientists and laypeople. (an event)
6. Many people who lived during the Victorian era were appalled when Darwin put forth the suggestion that their ancestry may have included apes.
7. In 1961 the U.S. government made the announcement that we would put the first man on the moon.
8. Nikita Khrushchev once advanced the claim that by 1975 communism would bury the system of capitalism.
9. In the 1960s the Supreme Court passed the rule that anyone under arrest for a crime that he or she may or may not have committed had to be given the widest possible benefit of legal doubt.
10. American prisons are for the most part schools for crime and pits of degradation.

In these next, prune the redundancy and the abstraction and create coordinate modifiers of your own devising. For example, here is a coordinate resumptive modifier built on to number 5 above:

> . . . ethical *issues* that are troubling both scientists and laymen, *issues* that yield easily to neither historical religious principles nor contemporary legal theory.

11. The general concept of systematic skepticism is in effect a kind of denial that there can ever be any kind of certain knowledge of reality screened and influenced by human perception.
12. The originating point when the field of scientific inquiry began to develop is to be found for the most part in the individual and personal observations of naive primitive peoples about the natural things that appear to occur in a regular way.
13. In the period known to scholars and historians as the Renaissance period, increases in affluence and stability in the area of political affairs had the practical consequence and outcome of allowing streams of thought of various different kinds to merge and flow together with one another.
14. During the recent period of about the last few years or so, we have been witness to a very large number of various specific acts and deeds that mainly involve terroristic components.

MOVEMENT AND MOMENTUM

A well-managed long sentence can be just as clear and as crisp as several short ones. A writer who can handle a long sentence gracefully lets us take a breath at reasonable intervals and at appropriate places; one part of the sentence will echo another with coordinated and parallel elements. And if he avoids muddling about in abstraction and weak passives, each sentence will move with the directness and energy that a readable style demands.

But if a sentence is to flow easily, its writer should also avoid making us hesitate over words and phrases that break its major grammatical links—subject-verb, verb-object. We should be able to complete all those links quickly and surely. Here, for example, is a sentence that does not flow:

> China, in order to exert in a more direct way its influence among the Eastern Bloc nations, in 1958 began in a carefully orchestrated manner a diplomatic offensive against the Soviet Union.

This flows more smoothly:

> In 1958, in order to exert a more direct influence among the Eastern Bloc nations, China began a carefully orchestrated diplomatic offensive against the Soviet Union.

Both sentences make us pause, but the first forces us to hold our breath after the subject, *China,* as we wait for the verb, *began;* the second lets us take a breath halfway through, when we finish the second introductory phrase, and then quickly connect the subject with its verb. The two versions differ only in the order of the phrases. In the first sentence, the important grammatical connections are broken; in the second, they are intact. And in the first, the phrases are ordered from longer to shorter; in the second, from shorter to longer.

Grammatical Connections

Normal English word order is subject-verb-object*. All things being equal, avoid breaking the connections between those parts. If you delay or muddy the subject-verb connection, your reader may hesitate, backtrack, reread looking for it. As a consequence, your reader will feel your style to be tense and uncertain.

Given that principle of "closure," we can explain why the second example sentence in the preceding section reads more easily than the first. In the second, nothing separates the subject from its verb or the verb from its object:

> (verb + object) In order to exert + a more direct influence
> (subject + verb) China + began
> (verb + object) began + a carefully orchestrated diplomatic offensive

But in the first version, the grammatical connections are interrupted:

> China [in order to exert . . . Eastern Bloc nations] began
> exert [in a more direct way] its influence
> began [in a carefully orchestrated manner] a diplomatic offensive

It is true that competent writers do interrupt the subject-verb link with phrases and clauses. And it is true that many short adverbs fit between subject and verb quite comfortably:

> Scientists the world over *deliberately* write in a style that is aloof, impersonal, and objective.

But longer phrases and clauses fit there less comfortably:

> Scientists the world over, *because they deliberately write in a style that is aloof, impersonal, and objective,* have difficulty communicating with laypeople.

If nothing else precedes the subject, you lose little by moving a long modifying phrase or clause to the beginning of its sentence:

> *Because scientists the world over deliberately write in a style that is aloof, impersonal, and objective,* they have difficulty communicating with laypeople.

When you place your modifier at the beginning of its sentence you avoid that flicker of hesitation which, repeated, may inappropriately break the flow.

Exercise 7–2

These sentences contain unfortunate interruptions. Correct the interruption and add a summative, resumptive, or free modifier of your own creation. Also edit to eliminate wordiness.

1. The construction of the Interstate Highway System, owing to the fact that Congress, on the occasion when it originally voted funds for it, did not anticipate the cost of inflation, has run into insoluble problems.
2. Such conduct or behavior, for whatever reasons proffered, is rarely not at least to some degree prejudicial to good order and discipline.
3. TV game shows, due to the fact that they have an appeal to the basic cupidity in us all, are just about the most popular shows that appear on daytime TV.
4. The merit selection of those who serve as judges, given the low quality and character of elected officials, is an idea whose time came long ago.
5. The field of high-energy physics, working with certain devices that can actually accelerate particles to a speed almost as fast as the speed of light, is exploring the ultimate nature and makeup of matter.
6. The continued and unabated emission of carbon dioxide gas into the atmospheric environment, unless there is a marked reduction prior to the end of the century, will eventually result in a change in the climate of the world as we know it today.
7. Only those individuals who are the rich, in the case that the government in advance of the next congressional election does not make any provisions for all political candidates for office to receive campaign funds, will, in large enough numbers to assure a wide selection of candidates, have the ability for seeking public office.
8. Insistence that there is no proof by scientific means of a certain causal link between the activity of smoking and various disease entities such as cardiac heart failure and malignant cancer conditions, despite the fact that there is a strong statistical correlation between the act of smoking and disease,

continues to be the official stated position and policy of the cigaret companies.

9. Medical science, in about the last half century or so, due to the fact of great strides being made in the detection and even anticipation of sicknesses and diseases that in the last half century would simply make an appearance in our midst to result in the terrible devastation of whole populations, now has a year in advance the capability for the early prediction of future outbreaks of disease entities such as influenza.

Small Connections

Sometimes we awkwardly split an adjective from the modifying phrase that follows it. We put the adjective before a noun it modifies, and we put the phrase that modifies the adjective after the noun:

> The accountant has given *as accurate **a projection** as any that could be provided.*

> We are facing *a more serious **decision** than what you described earlier.*

> A *close **relationship** to the one just discovered* is the degree to which *similar **genetic material** to that of related species* can be modified by *different **DNA chains** from the ones first selected by Adams and Walsh.*

> *Another **course of action** than the present one* is necessary to accumulate *sufficient **capital** to complete such **projects** as those you have described.*

In each case, the adjective—usually an adjective being compared— is split from its following phrase:

> as accurate . . . as any that could be provided
> more serious . . . than what
> close . . . to the one
> similar . . . to that
> different . . . from the ones
> another . . . than the present
> sufficient . . . to complete
> such . . . as those you

We can maintain an unbroken rhythm if we put the adjective *after* the noun, right next to the phrase that completes the adjective:

> The accountant has given **a projection** *as accurate as any that could have been provided.*

> We are facing **a decision** *more serious than what you described earlier.*

> **A relationship** *close to the one just discovered* is the degree to which **genetic material** *similar to that of related species* can be modified by **DNA chains** *different from the ones first selected by Adams and Walsh.*

> **A course of action** *other than the present one* is necessary to accumulate **capital** *sufficient to complete* **projects** *such as those you describe.*

Some of the adjectives that we most frequently split off from their modifying phrases are these: *more . . . than, less . . . than, other . . . than, as . . . as, similar . . . to, equal . . . to, identical . . . to, same . . . as, different . . . from, such . . . as, separate . . . from, distant . . . from, related . . . to, close . . . to, next . . . to, difficult . . . to, easy . . . to, necessary . . . to, sufficient . . . to, adequate . . . to.*

Exercise 7-3

Each of the following contains several adjective phrases awkwardly disjoined. Edit the passages to reunite the phrases and to make the style clearer and more direct.

1. The reason why an identical ecological impact statement to that submitted the previous year indicates that it will again be difficult data to evaluate is that there is still no independent verifying information from that which has been supplied by the applicant in our possession.
2. Under circumstances in which similar EKG readings are obtained to those obtained earlier, other conditions than cardiac insufficiency must come under suspicion. The same proce-

dures as those outlined in the previous section must be closely adhered to on the expectation that as effective results as those outlined there are to be achieved in such cases.

3. As a result of the reorganization of the marketing research division, more accurate information than that which has been received in the past should allow the identification of different populations from those that have been traditionally aimed at. This will be relatively easy information to process in analysis as a result of the fact that there has already been accumulated such demographic data as the average financial income, expenditure patterns, etc., for many different markets. As a result of all this, greater efficiency than that which we achieved in our earlier operation last year may be a reasonable expectation.

SOME PROBLEMS WITH MODIFIERS

Sentences can grow both long and confusing when we add several modifiers. And because the logical and grammatical connections between the modifier and the thing modified sometimes become unclear or ambiguous, we also risk confusing our readers.

Dangling Modifiers

A modifier "dangles" when its implied subject differs from the specific subject of the clause that follows it:

> In order to limit the spread of the infection, the entire area was sealed off.

(The implied subject of *limit,* some person, is different from the subject of the main clause, *the entire area.*)

> Resuming negotiations after a break of several days, the same issues confronted both the union and the company.

(The implied subject of *resuming, the union and the company,* is different from the subject of the main clause, *the same issues.*)

Constructions like these rarely interfere with clear communication. But since they cause some readers to hesitate for a moment, you ought to avoid them on general principles. Either rewrite the introductory phrase so that it has its own subject or make the subject of the main clause agree with the implied subject of the introductory phrase:

> In order for *us* to limit the spread of the infection, the entire area was sealed off.
> In order to limit the spread of the infection, *the police* sealed off the entire area.

> When *the union and the company* resumed negotiations, the same issues confronted them.
> Resuming negotiations after a break of several days, *the union and the company* confronted the same issues.

Some modifiers that seem to dangle are in fact acceptable. If either the modifier or the subject of the main clause is part of the metadiscourse*, the modifier will seem entirely appropriate to most readers:

> *In order to start the motor,* **it is essential** that the retroflex cam connecting rod be disengaged.

> **To summarize,** *unemployment* in the southern tier of counties remains the state's major economic and social problem.

Misplaced Modifiers

A second problem with modifiers is that sometimes they seem to modify two things, or the wrong thing. One kind of ambiguous modifier can refer either forward or back:

> Overextending oneself in strenuous physical activity *too frequently* results in a variety of physical ailments.
> We failed *entirely* to understand the complexities of the problem.

In each of these, the modifier can just as easily appear in an unambiguous position:

> Overextending oneself *too frequently* in strenuous exercise. . . .
> Overextending oneself in physical exercise results *too frequently* in a variety of physical ailments.

> We *entirely* failed to understand. . . .
> We failed to understand *entirely*. . . .

A second kind of ambiguity occurs when a modifier at the end of a clause or sentence can modify either a neighboring or a more distant phrase:

> Scientists have learned that their observations are as necessarily subjective as those in any other field *in recent years*.

We can move the modifier to a less ambiguous position:

> *In recent years,* scientists have learned that. . . .
> Scientists have learned that *in recent years,* their observations. . . .

In these cases, we can also use a resumptive modifier to make clear what a modifier is supposed to modify. In the next sentence, for example, what is it that dictates—the relationships, the components, or the process?

> It may be that there are relationships among the components of the process that would dictate one order rather than another.

A moment's thought suggests that the relationships dictate, but why should we cause our reader to pause even for a moment to understand how one idea connects to another? A resumptive modifier would make it clear:

> It may be that there are relationships among the components of the process, relationships that would dictate one order rather than another.

Pronoun reference. A long sentence can also create problems with pronoun reference. If there is the slightest chance that a pronoun will confuse your reader, don't hesistate to repeat the antecedent. And if you can conveniently make one of your nouns plural and another singular, you can use singular and plural pronouns to distinguish what you're referring to.

Compare these:

Physicians must never forget that *their patients* are vitally concerned about *their* treatment and *their* prognosis, but that *they* are often unwilling to ask for fear of what *they* will say.

A physician must never forget that *his patients* are vitally concerned about *their* treatment and *their* prognosis, but that *they* are often unwilling to ask for fear of what *he* will say.

(We'll take up the matter of the masculine *he* in Lesson Nine.)

EXERCISE 7-4

Rearrange the elements in these sentences so that they flow more easily.

1. The new barbarians display a response to intense aesthetic experience that takes the form of "Wow" usually, so far as their range of expressiveness is concerned.
2. I will now sketch the solar system as it was conceived by pre-Copernican astronomers ordinarily in simple outline for you.
3. Historians impose not just their private view of historical relevancy but the implied view of their whole social matrix on the past with little sense of scholarly bias.
4. We can perhaps if we study the psychoanalytic theories that Freud created for his scholarly and therefore largely male audience honestly and objectively in all their masculine assumptions understand why psychiatry has assigned the major source of a man's mental disorder to his mother so often.
5. The isolation of various clotting mechanisms in higher mammals is the next point.
6. The relation of individual objective bits of data to general principles applicable at all times and everywhere is a more important defining feature of the modern mind.
7. That Woodrow Wilson's refusal to take the leadership of the United States Senate into his confidence caused the defeat of the Versailles Treaty is universally acknowledged.
8. Two historically antagonistic chambers, a variety of hereditary and appointed senators whose responsibility in

administrative affairs is relatively slight making up one and an elective body that carries on the important legislative activities making up the other, constitute the legislative branch.

9. A virus which bears no known relation to any other form of protein-based life was discovered last year, though, in England.

10. That the need to monitor the flow of hard currency across national boundaries more carefully in the years to come is an equally pressing matter is just as important, in the opinion of most international monetary experts.

These sentences suffer from a variety of dangling, misplaced, ambiguous, and otherwise badly constructed or positioned modifiers. Correct them, and then edit the sentences in any other way you see fit.

11. Having no previous familiarity with the mechanism, metal deposit detection efforts by means of its use were met with a lack of positive results.

12. With every expectation of success, new efforts to resolve the differences that have resulted in interference with communication in a short time should be initiated.

13. Realizing that the undergraduate curriculum must be completely reevaluated in the next few weeks, proposals have suddenly appeared on the agenda that had received earlier discussion.

14. After making an audit of all internal operations in the summer of 1978 a second audit examined the record of foreign affiliates that had not been previously audited by their local headquarters.

SUMMING UP
Managing Long Sentences

1. Avoid writing long, rhythmically unbroken sentences consisting of one clause tacked on to another tacked on to another tacked on to another.

2.   To create a gracefully long sentence, use one or more of the following devices:

a.   Coordination

Besides the fact that no previous civilization has experienced such rapid alterations in the condition of daily life, the life of the mind has changed greatly too.

No previous civilization has experienced such rapid alterations *in the condition of daily life* or *in the life of the mind.*

b.   Resumptive modifiers

Our discovery that the earth was not at the center of the universe reshaped our understanding not only of where we are but of who we are, which was changed again by Darwin, and again by Freud, and again by Einstein.

Our discovery that the earth was not at the center of the universe reshaped *our understanding* not only of where we are but of who we are, *an understanding* that was changed again by Darwin, and again by Freud, and again by Einstein.

c.   Summative modifiers

Most business people and government officials have maintained that the only way out of our current energy crisis is to construct a massive synthetic fuel industry, which is rejected by those environmentalists who argue that we can achieve the same net result by equally massive investments in mass transportation and insulation.

Most business people and government officials have maintained that the only way out of our current energy crisis is to construct a massive synthetic fuel industry, *a position* rejected by those environmentalists who argue that we can achieve the same net result by equally massive investments in mass transportation and insulation.

d.   Free modifiers

The Dog Whelk is one of the most common snails found in the intertidal zone of the northern East Coast which proliferates in especially dense colonies on rocky shelves from Maine all the way to the Arctic Circle.

The Dog Whelk is one of the most common snails found in
the intertidal zone of the northern East Coast, *proliferating*
in especially dense colonies on rocky shelves from Maine all
the way to the Arctic Circle.

3. To keep up the momentum in a long sentence, do not interrupt
    links between subject and verb or verb and object:

The Protagoras, *despite its questionable logic and rather
superficial philsophical content,* **remains** one of Plato's
most dramatically appealing dialogues.

*Despite its questionable logic and rather superficial
philosophical content,* **the Protagoras remains** one of
Plato's most dramatically appealing dialogues.

On the other hand, if the object is very long and the interrup-
ting phrase is very short, put the modifier between the verb
and object.

Few politicians are willing to acknowledge that the bulk of the
electorate regards them essentially as parasites *even to themselves.*

Few politicians are willing to acknowledge *even to themselves* that
the bulk of the electorate regards them essentially as parasites.

4. Watch for modifiers that do not modify what you intend them
    to:

Re-examining the issues that had been earlier discussed, a new
perspective on them arose among the committee.

Re-examining the issues that it had earlier discussed, the committee
developed a new perspective on them.

International terrorism is a problem for which our system of
government had no good solution, because in order to deal with it
terrorists have to be the objects of sudden and unexpected pre-
emptive attacks directed at targets located in other countries that
must be obliterated quickly and without public debate.

International terrorism is a problem for which our system of
government has no good solution. In order to deal with foreign-
based terrorists, we have to direct sudden and pre-emptive attacks
at *targets* located in other countries, *targets* that must be
obliterated quickly and without public debate.

A Touch of Class

Anything is better than not to write clearly. There is nothing to be said against lucidity, and against simplicity only the possibility of dryness. This is a risk well worth taking when you reflect how much better it is to be bald than to wear a curly wig.

SOMERSET MAUGHAM

But clarity and brevity, though a good beginning, are only a beginning. By themselves, they may remain bare and bleak. When Calvin Coolidge, asked by his wife what the preacher had preached on, replied "Sin," and, asked what the preacher had said, replied "He was against it," he was brief enough. But one hardly envies Mrs. Coolidge.

F. L. LUCAS

There are two sorts of eloquence; the one indeed scarce deserves the name of it, which consists chiefly in laboured and polished periods, an over-curious and artificial arrangement of figures, tinselled over with a gaudy embellishment of words, . . . The other sort of eloquence is quite the reverse to this, and which may be said to be the true characteristic of the holy Scriptures; where the eloquence does not arise from a laboured and far-fetched elocution, but from a surprising mixture of simplicity and majesty, . . .

LAURENCE STERNE

L et's assume that you can now write clear, cohesive, and appropriately emphatic prose. That in itself would constitute a style of such singular distinction that most of us would be quite satisfied to achieve so much. But even though we might prefer bald clarity to the complexity of most institutional prose, the unrelenting simplicity of the plain style can finally become very flat and dry indeed, eventually arid. Its plainness invests prose with the blandness of unsalted meat and potatoes—honest fare to be sure, but hardly memorable and certainly without zest. Sometimes a touch of class, a flash of elegance, can mark the difference between forgettable Spartan prose and a well-turned phrase that fixes itself in the mind of a reader.

Now, I can't tell you how to be graceful and elegant in the same way I can tell you how to be clear and direct. What I *can* do is tell you about some of the devices that some graceful writers use. But that advice is, finally, about as useful as listing the ingredients a great cook uses in his bouillabaisse and then expecting anyone to make it. Knowing the ingredients and knowing how to use them is the difference between reading cookbooks and Cooking.

What follows describes a few ingredients of a modestly elegant style. How imaginatively and skillfully you use them is the difference between reading this book on writing, and Writing.

BALANCE AND SYMMETRY

We've already described how you can use coordination* to extend a sentence* beyond a few words. Coordination itself will grace a sentence with a movement more rhythmic and satisfying than that of a noncoordinate sentence or sentences.

Compare:[1]

Cheesecake TV such as "Charlie's Angels" and "Three's Company" appealed to men who needed the stimulation of beautiful bodies. Women liked these shows because they longed for the energy those bodies represented and their freedom.

[1]The curly braces will signal *a coordinated* set of words, phrases, or clauses.

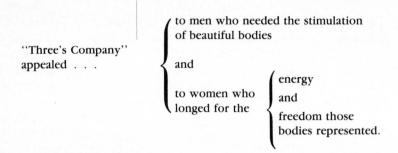

"Three's Company"
appealed . . .

to men who needed the stimulation
of beautiful bodies

and

to women who
longed for the

energy

and

freedom those
bodies represented.

We can enhance the rhythm and grace of coordination if we keep in mind a few simple principles. First, a coordinate series will move more gracefully if each succeeding coordinate element is longer than the one before it. So if you coordinate within a coordination, do it in the second element.

> The Sunbelt of southwestern states will continue to attract businesses looking for a low-salaried pool of nonunion labor and cheap energy and retirees looking for sunshine.

Schematically:

The Sunbelt of southwestern states will continue to attract

businesses looking for

and

retirees looking for sunshine.

a low-salaried pool of
nonunion labor

and

cheap energy,

Compare:

> The Sunbelt of southwestern states will continue to attract retirees looking for sunshine and businesses looking for cheap energy and a low-salaried pool of nonunion labor.

Schematically:

The Sunbelt of southwestern states will continue to attract

> {
>   retirees looking for sunshine
>   and
>   businesses looking for
> }
> {
>   cheap energy
>   and
>   a low-salaried pool of nonunion labor.
> }

In the second, the parallels move from shorter to longer, creating a rhythmically more attractive line.

We can use correlative conjunctions* such as *both X and Y, not only X but also Y, neither X nor Y* to signify a balanced coordination and to give it emphasis.

Compare these:

> The national significance of an ethnic minority depends upon a sufficiently deep historical identity that makes it
> {
>   impossible that the majority will absorb the minority
>   and
>   inevitable that the minority will
>   {
>   maintain its identity
>   and
>   transmit its heritage.
>   }
> }

> The national significance of an ethnic minority depends upon a sufficiently deep historical identity that makes it
> {
>   **not only** impossible that the majority will absorb the minority
>   **but**
>   inevitable that the minority will
>   {
>   **both** maintain its identity
>   **and**
>   transmit its heritage.
>   }
> }

The second is clearly stronger than the first.

You can make these coordinate patterns more rhetorically elegant if you consciously balance parts of phrases* and clauses* against one another:

Neither { the vacuous emotion of daytime soap opera
nor
the mindless eroticism of nighttime sitcoms

reflects the best { that American artists are able to create
or
that American audiences are willing to support.

The richest kind of balance and parallelism counterpoints both grammar and meaning: here *vacuous* is balanced against *mindless, emotion* against *eroticism, daytime* against *nighttime, soap opera* against *sitcoms, artists* against *audiences, able* against *willing,* and *create* against *support.*

You can achieve the same effect when you balance parts of sentences that are *not* coordinated. Here is a subject* balanced against an object*. The square brackets signal a balanced but not *coordinate* pair.

Scientists who tear down established views of the universe
invariably challenge
those of us who have built up our visions of reality upon
those views.

Here, the predicate* of a relative clause* in a subject is balanced against the predicate of that subject:

A government that is unwilling to
listen to the moderate voices of its citizenry
must eventually answer to the harsh justice of its revolutionaries.

A direct object balanced against the object of a preposition:

Those of us who are vitally concerned about our failing school systems are not quite ready to sacrifice
the intellectual growth of our innocent children
to
the social daydreaming of irresponsible bureaucrats.

Here is a main clause* balanced against a subordinate clause* and then a direct object and two prepositional objects balanced against one another:

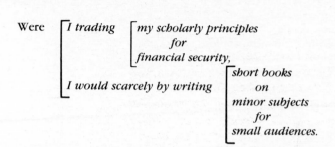

None of these are coordinated, but they are all consciously balanced. Like every other artful device, these balanced phrases and clauses can eventually become self-defeating—or at least monotonously arch. But if you use them unobtrusively when you want to emphasize an important point or conclude the line of an argument, you can give your prose a shape and a cadence that most ordinary writing lacks.

Exercise 8-1

Pick five or six sentences that have been laid out schematically in this lesson or in any of the previous lessons and imitate their structural patterns. Don't try to imitate the sentences word for word or even phrase for phrase, but do try to follow the general structural pattern of the example. For example, here's a sentence with a second coordination in the object:

A contemplative life in the country

> requires the energy to overcome the brute facts of an uncooperative Nature
> but
> rewards the person who has that energy
>> with the unmatchable satisfaction of having done it
>> and
>> with an inner confidence that makes contemplation meaningful.

First, think of a subject close enough to this one to make your imitation easy—for example, the academic life:

Life as a college professor
$\left\{\begin{array}{l}\text{offers summer vacations longer than most}\\ \text{but}\\ \text{imposes a sense of guilt on that person who}\end{array}\right.$
$\left\{\begin{array}{l}\text{ignores his or her scholarly work}\\ \text{and}\\ \text{enjoys the time the profession offers.}\end{array}\right.$

Try laying out your sentence in the way the model is schematically arranged, but then write it out in the usual way, so that you can get the feel of a long sentence as it unfolds before you.

Some of the sentences you might imitate are on pages 131–134, 154–157.

Here are the first halves of some balanced sentences. Finish them so that the last half balances against the first half.

1. Those who keep silent over the loss of small freedoms . . .
2. While the strong are never afraid to admit their real weaknesses, the weak . . .
3. We should pay more attention to those politicians who tell us how to make what we have better than to those . . .
4. When parents raise children who do not value the importance of hard work, the adults those children become . . .
5. Too many teachers mistake neat papers rehashing conventional ideas for . . .

In these next exercises, you have only the pattern. You invent the material. Use other verbs, if they allow you to follow the pattern.

6. trade X for Y (for example: I would never *trade* an immediate but transitory pleasure *for* a distant but enduring virtue.)
7. mistake X for Y
8. substitute X for Y
9. balance X against Y
10. sell X for Y

EMPHASIS AND RHYTHM

As we have seen, emphasis is largely a matter of controlling the way a sentence ends. When we maneuver our most important information into that stressed position, the natural emphasis we hear

in our mind's ear underscores the rhetorical emphasis of a significant idea. But the sentence will still seem weak and anticlimactic if
it ends with lightweight words.

Different parts of speech carry different weights. Prepositions are very light—one reason why we sometimes want to avoid
leaving a preposition at the end. Sentences should move toward
strength; a preposition can dilute that strength.

Compare:

> The intellectual differences among races is a subject that only the
> most politically indifferent scientist *is willing to look into.*

> The intellectual differences among races is a subject that only the
> most politically indifferent scientist *is willing to explore.*

Adjectives and adverbs are heavier than prepositions but
lighter than verbs and nouns. The heaviest, the most emphatic
words, are nominalizations*, those nouns derived from verbs and
adjectives. So if you want to end a sentence, or even a clause inside
a sentence, with the greatest emphasis, end with a nominalization
or with a phrase centered on a nominalization.

Compare these, the first version by Somerset Maugham:

> You would have thought that men who passed their lives in
> the study of the great masters of literature would be suffi-
> ciently sensitive to the beauty of language to write if not
> beautifully at least with perspicuity.

> You would have thought that men who passed their lives
> studying the great masters of literature would be sufficiently
> sensitive to beautiful language to write about it if not
> beautifully at least perspicuously.

In the second version, we've changed the indirect abstract
nominalizations to verbs, adjectives, and adverbs, words more immediate and direct—but at great cost to the concluding rhythm of
the sentence. In Maugham's original, each major segment ends
with a phrase built around a nominalization:

> in the *study* of the great masters of literature
> to the *beauty* of language
> with *perspicuity*

Another example: Which version is from Winston Churchill's "Finest Hour" speech is obvious.

> until in God's good time, the New World, with all its power and might, steps forth to the rescue and the liberation of the old.

> until in God's good time, the New World, with all its power and might, steps forth to rescue and liberate the old.

The second is weak, banal, pedestrian.

In fact, artfully placed nominalizations can elevate an otherwise flat style to one with a touch of elegance. Compare these two passages; one of them, from his *Memoirs,* is George Kennan's description of Averell Harriman. Which better reflects Harriman's own elegance is obvious:

> He had that curious contempt for elegance that only the wealthy can normally afford . . . in Moscow, [his] interest was, properly and commendably, the prospering of the American war effort and American diplomacy as President Roosevelt viewed and understood it. To the accomplishment of his part in the furtherance of this objective he addressed himself with a dedication, a persistence, and an unflagging energy and attention that has no parallel in my experience. . . . His physical frame, spare and sometimes ailing, seemed at best an unwelcome irrelevance. I had the impression that it was with an angry impatience that he took cognizance of the occasional reminders of its existence, dragged it with him on his daily rounds of duty, and forced it to support him where continuation without its support was not possible.

> He had that curious contempt for elegant things that only wealthy people can normally afford . . . in Moscow, he was interested, properly and commendably, only in helping the American war effort and American diplomacy as President Roosevelt viewed and understood it. To accomplish his part in this objective he addressed himself in a dedicated and persistent way, with an unflagging energy and attention that parallels nothing I have experienced. . . . His physical frame, spare and sometimes ailing, seemed at best unwelcome and irrelevant. It seemed to me that he was angrily im-

patient when he recognized those times when it reminded
him that it existed, dragged it with him on his daily rounds
of duty, and forced it to support him where he could not
have continued if it had not supported him.

Now, when a writer combines nominalizations with balanced
and parallel constructions, even redundantly parallel constructions, we know he is cranking up a style that is openly aiming at
elegant complexity. This sentence by Walter Lippmann is a good
example:

This shows that the {*preservation* and *defense*} of *freedom* of *opinion* is

{ not only a matter of *adhering* to abstract legal rights

but also, and very urgently,

a matter of {*organizing* and *arranging*} sufficient *debate*. }

Compare the less redundant but also less elegant,

> This shows that if we want to preserve free opinion, we
> must adhere to abstract legal rights and very urgently
> organize things so that we can debate issues sufficiently.

There is another rather small but important point of elegance: If
we seek an *extravagantly* elegant style, we can construct
elaborately balanced units, sprinkle them with nominalizations,
and end many of our sentences with phrases introduced by *of.*
Many such phrases result from nominalizations:

> . . . the preservation and defense *of freedom of opinion.*

Exercise 8-2

In addition to suffering from several other faults, these next
sentences end on weak adjectives and adverbs or clumsy
possessives. Change them so that they end on more heavily
stressed words, particularly on prepositional phrases beginning
with *of.* For example:

Our interest in ESP, UFOs, and other paranormal phenomena testifies to the fact that we have empty spirits and shallow minds.

Our interest in ESP, UFOs, and other paranormal phenomena testifies to the emptiness of our spirits and the shallowness of our minds.

1. Not very many tendencies in our governmental system have brought about more changes in American daily life than federal governmental agencies that are very powerful.
2. In the year 1923 several of the representatives from the side of the victorious Allied nations went to Versailles with the intention of seeking to dismember Germany's economic potential and to destroy her armaments industry.
3. The day is eliminated when school systems' boards of education have the expectation that local area taxpayers will automatically go along with whatever extravagant things administrators decide to do.
4. The blueprint for the political campaign plan was concocted by the mayor's advisers who are least sensitive.
5. If we invest our sweat in these projects, we must avoid appearing to be working only because we are interested in ourselves.
6. Irreplaceable works of native art are progressing into slow deterioration in many of our most prestigious museums for the reason that their curators have no recognition of how extremely fragile even recent artifacts can be.
7. Throughout history, science has made progress because dedicated scientists have gotten around a hostile public that is uninformed.

LENGTH AND RHYTHM

In ordinary prose, the length of your sentences becomes an issue only if they are all about fifteen words long or if they are all much longer, over thirty or so. Though one eighteen-to-twenty-word sentence after another isn't the ideal goal, they will seem less obviously monotonous than a series of sentences that are regularly and significantly longer or shorter.

In artful prose, on the other hand, length is more deliberately controlled. Some accomplished stylists can write one short sentence after another, perhaps to suggest a note of urgency:

Toward noon Petrograd again became the field of military
action; rifles and machine guns rang out everywhere. It was
not easy to tell who was shooting or where. One thing was
clear; the past and the future were exchanging shots. There
was much casual firing; young boys were shooting off
revolvers unexpectedly acquired. The arsenal was wrecked.
. . . Shots rang out on both sides. But the board fence
stood in the way, dividing the soldiers from the revolution.
The attackers decided to break down the fence. They broke
down part of it and set fire to the rest. About twenty barracks came into view. The bicyclists were concentrated in
two or three of them. The empty barracks were set fire to at
once.

> —Leon Trotsky, *The Russian Revolution* trans. by Max Eastman

Or terse certainty:

The teacher or lecturer is a danger. He very seldom
recognizes his nature or his position. The lecturer is a man
who must talk for an hour. France may possibly have acquired the intellectual leadership of Europe when their
academic period was cut down to forty minutes. I also have
lectured. The lecturer's first problem is to have enough
words to fill forty or sixty minutes. The professor is paid for
his time, his results are almost impossible to estimate.
. . . No teacher has ever failed from ignorance. That is em-
piric professional knowledge. Teachers fail because they
cannot "handle the class." Real education must ultimately
be limited to men who INSIST on knowing, the rest is mere
sheep-herding.

> —Ezra Pound, *ABC of Reading*

Or fire:

Let us look at this American artist first. How did he ever get
to America, to start with? Why isn't he a European still,
like his father before him?

Now listen to me, don't listen to him. He'll tell you the lie
you expect. Which is partly your fault for expecting it.

He didn't come in search of freedom of worship. England
had more freedom of worship in the year 1700 than America had. Won by Englishmen who wanted freedom and so

stopped at home and fought for it. And got it. Freedom of
worship? Read the history of England during the first
century of its existence.

Freedom anyhow? The land of the free! This the land of
the free! Why, if I say anything that displeases them, the
free mob will lynch me, and that's my freedom. Free? Why I
have never been in any country where the individual has
such an abject fear of his fellow countrymen. Because, as I
say, they are free to lynch him the moment he shows he is
not one of them. . . .

All right then, what did they come for? For lots of
reasons. Perhaps least of all in search of freedom of any
sort: positive freedom, that is.

— D.H. Lawrence, *Studies in Classic American Literature*

In this last example, Lawrence invests his discourse with even
more urgency by breaking sentences into fragments and what
could be longer paragraphs into snatches of discourse.

Equally accomplished writers write one long sentence after
another to suggest an inquiring mind exploring an idea:

In any event, up at the front of this March, in the first line,
back of that hollow square of monitors, Mailer and Lowell
walked in this barrage of cameras, helicopters, TV cars,
monitors, loudspeakers, and wavering buckling twisting line
of notables, arms linked (line twisting so much that at times
the movement was in file, one arm locked ahead, one
behind, then the line would undulate about and the other
arm would be ahead) speeding up a few steps, slowing
down while a great happiness came back into the day as if
finally one stood under some mythical arch in the great
vault of history, helicopters buzzing about, chop-chop, and
the sense of America divided on this day now liberated
some undiscovered patriotism in Mailer so that he felt a
sharp searing love for his country in this moment and on
this day, crossing some divide in his own mind wider than
the Potomac, a love so lacerated he felt as if a marriage were
being torn and children lost—never does one love so much
as then, obviously, then—and an odor of wood smoke, from
where you knew not, was also in the air, a smoke of dignity
and some calm heroism, not unlike the sense of freedom
which also comes when a marriage is burst—Mailer knew

for the first time why men in the front line of battle are almost always ready to die; there is a promise of some swift transit. . . .

    —Norman Mailer, *Armies of the Night*

The punctuated sentence goes on for several hundred more words.

Exercise 8-3

First, imitate a passage that has a series of very short sentences. Then imitate the Mailer sentence (you might want to read the rest of it in Book I, Part III, Chapter 4, of *Armies of the Night*). Then try to revise the passages made up of short sentences into just one or two long sentences, each in the style of Mailer. Then revise the Mailer passage into a series of short, curt sentences.

METAPHOR

Clarity, vigor, symmetry, rhythm—prose so graced would more than satisfy most of us. And yet, if it offered no virtues other than these, such prose would excite an admiration only for our craft, not for the reach of our imagination. This next passage displays all the stylistic graces we've described so far, but it goes beyond mere craftsmanship. It reveals a truth about pleasure through a figure of speech embedded in a comparison that is itself almost metaphorical.

> The secret of the enjoyment of pleasure is to know when to stop. . . . We do this every time we listen to music. We do not seize hold of a particular chord or phrase and shout at the orchestra to go on playing it for the rest of the evening; on the contrary, however much we may like that particular moment of music, we know that its perpetuation would interrupt and kill the movement of the melody. We understand that the beauty of a symphony is less in these musical moments than in the whole movement from beginning to end. If the symphony tries to go on too long, if at a certain point the composer exhausts his creative ability and tries to

carry on just for the sake of filling in the required space of
time, then we begin to fidget in our chairs, feeling that he
has denied the natural rhythm, has broken the smooth curve
from birth to death, and that though a pretense of life is being made, it is in fact a living death.
    —Alan W. Watts, *The Meaning of Happiness*

Watts could have written this:

. . .however much we may like that particular moment of
music, we know that its perpetuation would interrupt and
spoil the movement of the melody. . . . we begin to fidget
in our chairs, feeling that he has denied the natural rhythm,
has interrupted the regular movement from beginning to end,
and that though a pretense of wholeness is being made, it is
in fact a repeated end.

The two passages are equally clear and graceful. But the first
illuminates music—and pleasure—in a way the second does not.
The metaphor of birth and the smooth, unbroken curve of life into
death startles us with a flash of unexpected truth.
    Of metaphor, Aristotle wrote,

By far the greatest thing is to be a master of metaphor. It is
the one thing that cannot be learned from others. It is a sign
of genius, for a good metaphor implies an intuitive perception of similarity among dissimilars.

A metaphor invites us to see a familiar thing in a new way. Similes
do the same, but less intensely, the *like* or *as* moderating the force
of the comparison.
    Compare these:

The schoolmaster is the person who takes the children off
the parents' hands for a consideration. That is to say, he
establishes a child prison, engages a number of employee
schoolmasters as turnkeys, and covers up the essential cruelty and unnaturalness of the situation by torturing the
children if they do not learn, and calling this process, which

is within the capacity of any fool or blackguard, by the
sacred name of Teaching.
    —G. B. Shaw, *Sham Education*

. . . he establishes something like a child prison, engages a
number of employee schoolmasters to act like turnkeys,
covers up the essential cruelty and unnaturalness of the
situation by doing things to the children that are like torture
if they do not learn. . . . calling this process, which is
within the capacity of any fool or blackguard, by the sacred
name of Teaching.

Both passages say essentially the same thing about education, but
the first with more intensity and immediacy.

You may think that metaphor is appropriate only to poetic
writing, or reflective or polemical writing. But metaphor vivifies
all kinds of prose. Many historians rely on it:

This is what may be called the common-sense view of
history. History consists of a corpus of ascertained facts.
The facts are available to the historian in documents, in-
scriptions, and so on, like fish on the fishmonger's slab. The
historian collects them, takes them home, and cooks and
serves them in whatever style appeals to him. Acton, whose
culinary tastes were austere, wanted them served plain.
. . . Sir George Clark, critical as he was of Acton's attitude,
himself contrasts the "hard core of facts" in history with
the "surrounding pulp of disputable interpretation"—forget-
ting perhaps that the pulpy part of the fruit is more reward-
ing than the hard core.
    —E. H. Carr, *What Is History?*

So do biologists:

Some of you may have been thinking that, instead of
delivering a scientific address, I have been indulging in a
flight of fancy. It is a flight, but not of mere fancy, nor is it
just an individual indulgence. It is my small personal attempt
to share in the flight of the mind into new realms of our
cosmic environment. We have evolved wings for such
flights, in the shape of the disciplined scientific imagination.
Support for those wings is provided by the atmosphere of

> knowledge created by human science and learning: so far as
> this supporting atmosphere extends, so far can our wings
> take us in our exploration.
>> —Julian Huxley, "New Bottles for Old Wine," *Journal of the Royal Anthropological Institute*

And philosophers:

> Suppose I look at the night sky through a piece of heavily
> smoked glass on which certain lines have been left clear.
> Then I shall see only the stars that can be made to lie on the
> lines previously prepared upon the screen, and the stars I do
> see will be seen as organized by the screen's structure. We
> can think of a metaphor as such a screen. We can say that
> the principal subject is "seen through" the metaphorical ex-
> pression—or, if we prefer, that the principal subject is "pro-
> jected upon" the field of the subsidiary subject.
>> —Max Black, "Metaphor," *Models and Metaphors*

And when they are writing of new ideas for which there is yet no standard language, so do physicists:

> Whereas the lepton pair has a positive rest mass when it is
> regarded as a single particle moving with a velocity equal to
> the vector sum of the motions of its two components, a
> photon always has zero rest mass. This difference can be
> glossed over, however, by treating the lepton pair as the off-
> spring of the decay of a short-lived photonlike parent called
> a virtual photon.
>> —Leon M. Lederman, "The Upsilon Particle," *Scientific American*

These metaphors serve different ends. Shaw used prison to emphasize a point that he could have made without it. But prisons, turnkeys, and torture invest his argument with an emotional inten- sity that ordinary language could not communicate. Carr used fish and fruit both to emphasize and to illuminate. He could have ex- pressed his ideas more prosaically, but the literal statement would have been longer and weaker. Black and Lederman used their com- parisons not to emphasize but entirely to explain; neither required any dramatically heightened emphasis.

But if metaphor can sometimes evidence a fresh imagination, it can also betray those of us whose verbal imaginations fall short of the metaphor's demands. Too often, we use metaphor to gloss over inexact thinking:

> Societies give birth to new values through the differential osmotic flow of daily social interaction. Conflicts evolve when new values collide with the old, a process that frequently spawns yet a new set of values that synthesize the conflict into a reconciliation of opposites.

We get the idea, but through a cracked glass of careless metaphor. The birth metaphor suggests a traumatic event, but the new values, it is claimed, result from osmotic flow, a process constituted by a multitude of invisibly small events. Conflicts do not usually "evolve"; they more often occur in an instant, as suggested by the metaphor of collision. The spawning image picks up the metaphor of birth again, but by this time the image is, at best, collectively ludicrous.

Had the writer thought through his ideas carefully, he might have expressed them in clearer, nonfigurative language:

> As we continuously interact with one another in small ways, we gradually create new social values. When one person behaves according to one of these new values and another according to an old value, the values may come into conflict, creating a new third value that reconciles the other two.

Less misleading, but more embarrassing, are those passages that confuse emphasis with extravagance. Huxley's passage about the wings of inquiry flapping in an atmosphere of scientific knowledge comes perilously close. This next topples over into bathos:

> The slavering maw of inflation is wolfing down the hard-earned savings of retired people. As they plummet headlong into the pit of penury, they see before them only the prospect of economic perdition.

Metaphors also invite trouble if we aren't sensitive to their earlier incarnations. Many words that we use altogether prosaically originated in dead metaphors that spring back to life when we least expect it. We "look over" a problem in order to "handle" it correctly. Once we "grasp" its difficulty, we can "break" the problem down into its parts. None of these metaphors is remarkable in any way; indeed, we are not even conscious of their being metaphors. But when we conjoin dead metaphors carelessly, we can unwittingly—and often ludicrously—resurrect their earlier meanings.

> Unless marketing research can get a feel for the tastes of the
> younger buyer, the thrust of any advertising campaign will
> be fruitless.

We can get an idea about tastes, or a feel for preferences; the thrust of a campaign may be in the wrong direction; or an effort can be fruitless. But a "feel" for a "taste" is as obscenely silly as a "fruitless thrust."

Sad to say, there are no simple rules for distinguishing good metaphors from bad. About the only safe rule is this: If you create a metaphor that makes you feel good every time you read it, cut it out. It's sure to be too clever by half. And if you discover yourself chasing a metaphor through more than two lines, as Huxley did, start over.

It's tempting to advise struggling writers never to use metaphors: we can write clearly, persuasively, even movingly without them. But those who seek a prose style that is more than merely clear and concise might keep in mind what Dr. Johnson once said of Jonathan Swift: "The rogue never hazards a metaphor." Swift was one of the great prose craftsmen of English literature, and in fact he ventured more than a few metaphors. But Johnson was right, too: For all his stylistic wit and brilliance, Swift lacked that flash of imagery and metaphor that makes memorable the prose of some others who could not construct a sentence half so well.

As with a sense of elegance and grace, developing a good ear—or eye—for metaphor takes practice. And perhaps Aristotle was right, too: Perhaps it cannot be learned at all. But the rewards of learning how to handle metaphor go beyond a style that is merely a bit more mannered than usual. Metaphor is a way of exploring a subject, a way of seeing a subject through a prism of new perspectives.

Writers just beginning to experiment with metaphor will fail more often than they will succeed. Almost invariably, whenever we learn a new skill, we exercise its particular virtues to excess: When we first learn to drive, we steer too much; after a course in logic, we attempt to construct every argument out of rigorous syllogisms. And in matters of style, those who master a new device, a new turn of phrase, will use it everywhere. Unfortunately, failed first attempts at metaphoric elegance are more glaring than exaggerated efforts toward clarity and simplicity. And so those entirely natural, entirely predictable early failures can embarrass and discourage even the most diligent students of style. I can only reassure those who are chagrined by their early infelicities that everyone experiences the same failures, that no one has ever easily achieved elegant simplicity, much less effortless elegance.

Exercise 8-4

The following sentences exhibit excessive length, pervasive wordiness, and some unfortunate metaphors. Edit them in whatever ways you think appropriate.

1. I would like to state that the various figures that are contained in the first quarter report that in effect seem to spell out particular numbers of importance in regard to the facts regarding productivity, particularly the hidden and unseen costs that are clearly a reflection of as yet unseen renewed pressures of an inflationary origin that are throwing a monkey wrench into our research budget, reveal the considerable degree to which we are in special need of research efforts and activities into new and innovative approaches to a way out of the skyrocketing spiral of wages and compensation for labor that is usually classed as unskilled.
2. In order that a solid grasp of the abstract heart of Einstein's theory of relativity be mastered, there is the initial necessity as to seeing the speed of light as a constant factor, regardless of and independent of where the observer rests or what the particular speed of any given observer might perhaps be in relationship to any other object that may be found in the universe, which is an intellectual leap that escapes a great many people.

3. It is certainly the case there should not be the setting of one's sights with too great a reliance in the hope that we are creatures of a rational order who have the capability of molding the emptiness of the vast universe into an element of a deep picture of our relationship to basic and fundamental existence, due to the fact that we are still in possession of many of the animal-type drives that stop us from logical though processes as to the fact that immortality is not a spoke in the wheel of transient existence.

SUMMING UP
A Bit of Flair

The most obvious traits of a modestly elegant style include both syntactic patterns and a choice of words that raise the passage above the ordinary. But most important, true stylistic elegance demands a quality of thought that makes a reader feel he is confronting a writer of substantial intellectual quality.

I can't tell you how to be a writer of substantial intellectual quality. Nor can I list all the words that would invest your prose with any special distinction. About the best I can do here is list a few of the sentence patterns that you might experiment with when you believe your ideas merit special attention.

1. Balanced, coordinate, and parallel sentence patterns, more often after the subject than before the verb, with elements of increasing length.
2. Nominalizations toward the end of a clause, concluding with a sprinkling of prepositional phrases introduced by *of.*
3. Few, if any, sequences of N + N + N . . .
4. A few patterns of usage to signal your audience you are raising your prose to a level of formality that should command their attention. (See the next Lesson.)

Style and Usage

It is not the business of grammar, as some critics seem preposterously to imagine, to give law to the fashions which regulate our speech. On the contrary, from its conformity to these, and from that alone, it derives all its authority and value.

GEORGE CAMPBELL

No grammatical rules have sufficient authority to control the firm and established usage of language. Established custom, in speaking and writing, is the standard to which we must at last resort for determining every controverted point in language and style.

HUGH BLAIR

English usage is sometimes more than mere taste, judgment, and education—sometimes it's sheer luck, like getting across the street.

E. B. WHITE

So far, we've discussed matters of choice: From among sentences that might all express the same idea, how do we pick the best one? We might reject

> There was an insufficiency of comptroller research support.

for

> The comptroller did not support our research sufficiently.

But we wouldn't say that the first was grammatically wrong, only less forceful and direct than it could be.

At first glance, we might think grammar and usage to be altogether different. When we read in the *American Heritage Dictionary* that *irregardless* is "nonstandard . . . never acceptable" (except when we're trying to be funny), the possibility of choosing between *irregardless* and *regardless* may seem at best academic. *Regardless* versus *irregardless* isn't a matter of better and worse but of right and utterly, irredeemably wrong.

That seems to simplify matters: To choose correctly, we don't need good taste or sound judgment, only a reliable memory. If we remember that *enthuse* is always and everywhere wrong, then *enthuse* does not even rise to the level of conscious decision. We have only to memorize the same kind of prescriptions for a host of other items:

— Don't begin a sentence* with *and* or *but*.
— Don't end a sentence with a preposition*.
— Don't split infinitives*.
— Don't use double negatives.

Unfortunately, questions of usage are not quite that simple: A good many of the grammatical rules we find in some dictionaries and in some handbooks of usage have little or no basis in linguistic fact. Other social rules of usage are imperatives that we violate at the risk of seeming at least badly educated. And then there are rules that we can observe or not, depending on the effect we want.

It's important to keep in mind that in this book we're discussing not spoken, but written English. The English-speaking world has a great variety of spoken dialects, each different from the others in pronunciation, vocabulary, and grammar. Despite what some may think about a "pure Boston English" as opposed to "illiterate Ozark," no local spoken dialect is inherently better—or worse—than the standard dialect spoken in any other part of our country. Every region has a prestige dialect that careful speakers use on those occasions when careful speech is important. And each dialect has its own distinctive features of pronunciation, word choice, and grammar.

But written English is different. For better or worse, all parts of the English-speaking world have tacitly agreed on most of the conventions that define careful standard written English. Different parts of the native English-speaking world may spell a few words in different ways: *theatre* versus *theater, gaol* versus *jail, colour* versus *color,* and so on. We may differ on a very few small points of grammar: I *have no money* versus I *don't have any money.* And in different parts of the world, we may have different words for roughly the same things: *dust bin* versus *garbage can, attorney* and *barrister* versus *lawyer,* and so on. But for the most part, native speakers of English observe a written standard that is far more uniform than the standard among local spoken dialects. This development of a written standard occurs in every literate society.

rules and RULES

To the end of creating this standard written English, grammarians and teachers of English have, over the last few hundred years, assembled a variety of prescriptions and proscriptions whose observance, they believe, distinguishes writers who are careful and responsible from those who are not. The rules range from where to put a comma, to how to use *disinterested* and *uninterested,* to the proper case of a pronoun after *is.* But these rules have been hoarded up less on the basis of their intrinsic logical force or on principles of inherent clarity and precision, than on grounds that have been largely idiosyncratic, historically accidental. No universal principle of logic or experience demands that the past tense of *know* be *knew* rather than *knowed,* or that *like* be now and forevermore a preposition, never a conjunction.

As one consequence of this largely random accumulation, not all rules of usage have equal standing with all writers of English, even all careful writers of English. A very few especially fastidious writers and editors have accepted and try to observe every rule. Most careful writers observe fewer, because they have never had all the rules imposed on them by all their editors or teachers, no matter how critical and careful those writers might be in other matters. There are also writers who know the rules, but who also know that not all of them are worth observing and that other rules should be observed only on certain occasions.

Whether we choose to be absolutely safe or rhetorically selective depends on both our competence and our confidence. We could adopt the worst case approach: We learn and observe all the rules all the time because somewhere, sometime, someone might condemn us for beginning a sentence with *and* or ending it with *up,* and so we keep a stack of grammar books and usage manuals close by to consult as we edit—painfully—every line we write, until we have memorized their rules so thoroughly that we obey them without thought. But once we do that, we may have deprived ourselves of a valuable stylistic flexibility. And sooner or later, we will impose all those rules—valid or not—on others. After all, what good is learning a rule if all we can do is obey it?

But careful selectivity has its problems too, because that requires us to learn which rules to ignore and which to observe—and when. It also demands the confidence to face up to those who consider a deliberately split infinitive or a singular *data* as a sign of careless writing—or deliberate scorn of careful writing.

An attitude short of blind obedience to every rule in every grammar book need not indicate a bad education or a contemptuous mind: We may reject some rules once we recognize how the best writers write—not how they *say* they write, but how they *do* write. If otherwise careful, educated, and intelligent writers of first-rate prose do not avoid ending a sentence with a preposition, then regardless of what some grammarians or editors would say, a preposition at the end of a sentence is *not* an error of usage.

The standard adopted here is not that of Transcendental Correctness. It derives from the observable habits of those we could never accuse of having sloppy minds or of deliberately writing careless prose. On the basis of that principle, we can recognize four kinds of "rules." The kinds are simple enough: What's less clear is which rules go in which category.

Real Rules

The first—the most important—category of rules includes those whose violation would unequivocally brand you as a writer of nonstandard English. Here are a few:

1. Double negatives: The engine had *hardly no* systematic care.
2. Nonstandard verb forms: They *knowed* that nothing would happen.
3. Double comparatives: This procedure is *more better*.
4. Some adjectives* for adverbs*: They did the work *real good*.
5. Redundant subjects*: *These ideas, they* need explanation.
6. Certain incorrect pronoun forms: *Him* and *me* will study the problem.
7. Some subject-verb disagreements: *They was* ready to begin.

There are others. But they are so egregious that most of you already know that they are never violated by educated writers. And because these rules are observed in even casual writing, their observance passes unremarked: They is rules whose violation we instantly notes, but whose observance we entirely ignore.

Nonrules

A second group of rules includes those whose observance we do not remark, and whose violation we do not remark either. In fact, these are not rules at all, but a species of folklore, widely enforced by editors and school teachers, but largely ignored by most educated and careful writers. What follows is based on a good deal of time spent reading prose that is carefully written and intended to be carefully read. I can only assert that the so-called rules listed below are violated so consistently that, unless we indict for bad grammar just about every serious writer of modern English, we have to reject as misinformed anyone who would try to enforce them.[1]

---

[1]Each citation offered as an example of a "rule" violated is in its original form, except for the italics, which I have added.

1.   "Never begin a sentence with a coordinating conjunction*
such as *and* or *but.*" Allegedly, not this:

> *But,* it will be asked, is tact not an individual gift, therefore
> highly variable in its choices? *And* if that is so, what
> guidance can a manual offer, other than that of its author's
> prejudices—mere impressionism?
> > —Wilson Follett, *Modern American Usage: A Guide,* edited
> > and completed by Jacques Barzun et al.

2.   "Never begin a sentence with *because.*" Allegedly, not this:

> *Because* we have access to so much historical fact, today we
> know a good deal about changes within the humanities
> which were not apparent to those in any age much before
> our own and which the individual scholar must constantly
> reflect on.
> > —Walter Ong, S. J., "The Expanding Humanities and the In-
> > dividual Scholar," *PMLA*

but presumably this:

> *Since* we have access to so much historical fact, today we. . . .

or

> We have access to much historical fact. *Consequently* today
> we. . . .

Although this proscription appears in no handbook of usage I
know of, it seems to have popular currency. It must stem from advice intended to avoid sentence fragments like this one:

> The application was rejected. *Because the deadline had passed.*

When the *because*-clause that opens a sentence is followed by a
main clause, and punctuated so that the two constitute a single
punctuated sentence, then it is entirely correct:

> *Because* the deadline had passed, the application was rejected.

3. "When referring to an inanimate referent, use the relative pronoun *that*—not *which*—for restrictive* clauses; use *which* for nonrestrictive clauses." Allegedly not this:

> Next is a typical situation *which* a practiced writer corrects "for style" virtually by reflex action.
>
> Jacques Barzun, *Simple and Direct*

But presumably this:

> Next is a typical situation *that* a practiced writer corrects "for style" virtually by reflex action.

Both are entirely correct.

4. "Use *each other* to refer to two, *one another* to refer to three or more." Allegedly, not this:

> Now "society" is ever in search of novelty—and it is a limited body of well-to-do women and men of leisure. From the almost exclusive association of these persons with *each other,* there arises a kind of special vocabulary, which is constantly changing. . . .
>
> —James B. Greenough and George L. Kittredge, *Words and Their Ways in English Speech*

But presumably this:

> From the almost exclusive association of these persons with *one another,* there arises a kind of special vocabulary. . . .

One another may be just a shade more formal than *each other,* but neither phrase is, in good usage, limited in the way the rule states.

5. "Use *between* with two, *among* with three or more." Allegedly, not this:

> . . . government remained in the hands of fools and adventurers, foreigners and fanatics, who *between* them went near to wrecking the work of the Tudor monarchy. . . .
>
> —Geo. Macaulay Trevelyan, *A Shortened History of England*

But presumably this:

> . . . government remained in the hands of fools and adven-
> turers, foreigners and fanatics, who *among* them went near
> to wrecking the work of the Tudor monarchy. . . .

Among goes with three or more, of course, but *between* also occurs in that context.

6. "Don't use *which* or *this* to refer to a whole clause."
Allegedly, not this:

> Although the publishers have not yet destroyed the plates of
> the second edition of Merriam-Webster's unabridged dic-
> tionary, they do not plan to keep it in print, *which* is a pity.
> —Dwight MacDonald, "The String Untuned," *The New Yorker*

But presumably this:

> Although the publishers have not yet destroyed the plates
> of . . . they do not plan to keep it in print, *a decision which* is a
> pity.

Occasionally, this kind of construction can be ambiguous. In the
next example, is it the letter that makes her happy, or the fact that
it was given to her?

> We gave her the letter, which made her happy.

Here, a summative modifier makes the meaning unambiguous:

> We gave her the letter, *a thoughtful act* that made her happy.

When it is clear what the *which* refers to, this kind of broad
reference is entirely acceptable.

7. "Use *fewer* with nouns you can count, *less* with quantities you
cannot." Allegedly, not this:

> I can remember no *less than five occasions* when the cor-
> respondence columns of The Times rocked with volleys of
> letters from the academic profession protesting that

academic freedom is in danger and the future of scholarship
threatened.

> —Noel Gilroy Annan, Lord Annan, "The Life of the Mind in
> British Universities Today," *ACLS Newsletter*

But presumably this:

> I can remember no *fewer than five occasions* when. . . .

It is true that *fewer* is restricted to countable nouns. But *less* now
frequently occurs with countable nouns in the prose of many who
certainly qualify as careful writers.

8. "Use *due to,* meaning 'because of,' only to introduce a phrase
    modifying a noun, never to introduce a phrase that modifies a
    verb." Allegedly, not this:

> . . . cooperation between the Department of Economics
> and the Business School and between the Business School
> and the Law School will be much greater ten years from
> now than at present, *due to* the personal relations of the
> younger men on the three faculties.
>
> —James Bryant Conant, The *President's Report: 1951–1952,*
> Harvard University Press

But presumably this:

> . . . cooperation will be much greater ten years from now
> than at present, *because of* the personal relations of the
> younger men on the three faculties.

There are also a few individual words whose usage is pro-
scribed by extremely conservative teachers and editors. But the actual use of these words by careful writers is, as a rule, unremarked
by equally careful readers. Most careful writers use *since* with the
meaning of "because"; *alternative* to refer to one of three or more
choices; *anticipate* to mean "expect"; *continuous* for *continual*
and vice versa: *contact* as a general verb meaning "communicate
with." Though *data* and *media* as singulars are *bêtes noires* for
some observers, they are used as singular nouns by large numbers
of careful writers, in the same way they use *agenda* and *insignia.*
(Strata, errata, and *criteria* still seem to be plurals for most
careful writers.) *Infer* for *imply* and *disinterested* for *uninterested*

are countenanced by some standard dictionaries whose editors base their decisions on the usage of careful writers. Many teachers and editors disagree.

In the most formal of circumstances, circumstances in which you would want to avoid the slightest hint of violating even the most trivial point of usage, you might decide to observe these rules (excepting 1 and 2). In most ordinary circumstances, though, they are ignored by most careful writers. If you decide to adopt the worst-case approach and observe them all, all the time—well, to each his own. Private virtues are their own reward.

Optional Rules

These next rules complement the first group: For the most part, few readers will notice if you violate them. But when you observe them, you will signal a level of formality that few careful readers will miss.

1. "Never split an infinitive." Some purists would condemn Dwight MacDonald, a linguistic archconservative, for writing this:

   > . . . one wonders why Dr. Gove and his editors did not think of labelling *knowed* as substandard right where it occurs, and one suspects that they wanted *to slightly conceal* the fact or at any rate to put off its exposure as long as decently possible.
   > —"The String Untuned," *The New Yorker*

They would require this:

   > . . . one wonders why Dr. Gove and his editors did not think of labelling *knowed* as substandard right where it occurs, and one suspects that they wanted *to conceal the fact slightly* or at any rate to put off its exposure as long as decently possible.

But the split infinitive is now so common among the very best writers that when we make an effort to avoid splitting it, we invite notice, whether we intend to or not.

2. "Use *shall* as the first person simple future, *will* for second and third person simple future; use *will* to mean strong intention in the first person, *shall* for second and third person." Some purists would condemn F. L. Lucas for writing this:

> I *will* end with two remarks by two wise old women of the civilized eighteenth century.
> —"What is Style?" *Holiday*

They would demand:

> I *shall* end with two remarks by two wise old women of the civilized eighteenth century.

They would be mistaken to do so.

3. "Always use *whom* as the object of a verb or preposition." Purists would condemn William Zinsser for writing this:

> Soon after you confront this matter of preserving your identity, another question will occur to you: *"Who* am I writing for?"
> —*On Writing Well*

They would insist on:

> Soon after you confront this matter of preserving your identity, another question will occur to you: "For *whom* am I writing?"

Whom is a small but distinct flag of conscious correctness, especially when the *whom* is in fact wrong:

> We found a candidate *whom* we thought was most qualified.

The rule: The form of the pronoun depends on whether it is a subject or an object of its own clause. Since *who* is the subject of *was* in

> We found a candidate ⎣ we thought *who* ⎦ was most qualified.

who is the correct form, not *whom*. In this next example, *whom* is the object of *overlooked:*

> We found a candidate ⎰ we thought we had overlooked.   *whom*

If you are in doubt about the matter, try dropping the *who/whom* altogether:

> We found a candidate we thought we had overlooked.

4.   "Never end a sentence with a preposition." Purists, presumably, would condemn Sir Ernest Gowers for this:

> The peculiarities of legal English are often used as a stick to beat the official *with*.
>   —*The Complete Plain Words*

And insist on this:

> The peculiarities of legal English are often used as a stick *with which* to beat the official.

The second is more formal than the first, but the first is still grammatically correct. In fact, whenever we move a preposition before its object, we make the sentence a bit more formal. And any obligatory *whom* after the preposition only compounds the formality.
  Compare:

> The man *with whom* I spoke was not the man *to whom* I had been referred.

> The man I spoke *with* was not the man I had been referred *to*.

5.   "Do not use *whose* as the possessive pronoun for an inanimate referent." Purists would correct I. A. Richards for writing this:

And, on other occasions, the meaning comes from other
partly parallel uses, *whose* relevance we can feel, without
necessarily being able to state it explicitly.
—*The Philosophy of Rhetoric*

They would change it to this:

And, on other occasions, the meaning comes from other partly
parallel uses, the relevance *of which* we can feel, without necessarily being able to state it explicitly.

6. "Use *one* as a generalized pronoun instead of *you.*" Purists
would edit Monroe Beardsley's:

When explicit meanings are wrongly combined, *you* get a
logical fault (this is oversimplifying somewhat, but take it as
a first approximation).
—"Style and Good Style," *Reflections on High School
English: NDEA Institute Lectures,* ed. Gary Tate

Into the more stilted:

When explicit meanings are wrongly combined, *one* gets a
logical fault (this is oversimplifying somewhat, but *one* may
take it as a first approximation).

7. "Do not refer to *one* with *he* or *his;* repeat *one.*" Purists
would deplore Theodore Bernstein's usage:

Thus, unless one belongs to that tiny minority who can
speak directly and beautifully, *one* should not write as *he*
talks.
—*The Careful Writer*

They would prefer the more formal:

Thus, unless *one* belongs to that tiny minority who can
speak directly and beautifully, *one* should not write as *one*
talks.

8. "When expressing a contrary-to-fact statement, use the subjunctive form of the verb. Purists would deny H. W. Fowler this:

> Another suffix that is not a living one, but is sometimes
> treated as if it *was,* is *-al;* &. . . .
> —*A Dictionary of Modern English Usage*

They would insist upon:

> Another suffix that is not a living one, but is sometimes
> treated as if it *were,* is *-al;* &. . . .

As the English subjunctive quietly fades into linguistic history, it leaves a residue of forms infrequent enough to impart to a sentence a slightly archaic—and therefore formal—tone. We regularly use the simple past tense to express most subjunctives:

> If we *knew* what to do, we *would* do it.

Be is the problem: Strictly construed, the subjunctive demands *were,* but *was* is gradually replacing it:

> If this *were* 1941, a loaf of bread would cost twenty cents.

> If this *was* 1941, a loaf of bread would cost twenty cents.

Certainly, when the occasion calls for sonorous formal English, the wise writer chooses the more formal usage. But in all these cases, the writer **chooses.**

Special Formality

The list of items that create a special sense of formality might include a few that don't involve disputed points of usage, but do let you elevate your style a bit above the ordinary.

1. Negative inversion. Probably the most famous negative inversion is President John F. Kennedy's

Ask not what your country can do for you, ask what you can do for your country.

Compare:

Do not ask what your country can do for you, . . .

Negatives such as *rarely, never, not, only,* and so on, typically let you put an auxilliary verb before its subject:

Never have so many owed so much to so few.

Rarely do we confront a situation such as this.

Only once has this corporation failed to pay a dividend.

2. Conditional inversion. Instead of beginning a conditional clause with *if,* begin it with *should, were,* or *had.*

Compare:

If anyone should question the grounds on which this decision was made, we can point to centuries of tradition.

Should anyone question the grounds on which this decision was made, we can point to centuries of tradition.

If there had been any objections, they would have been met.

Had there been any objections, they would have been met.

If I were prepared to answer you now, I should do so happily.

Were I prepared to answer you now, I should do so happily.

3. Instead of *do not have to,* use *need not:*

You *don't have to* answer now.

You *need not* answer now.

4. Instead of *does not have* any, use *have no:*

The court *does not have* any precedent to follow.

The court *has no* precedent to follow.

Bêtes Noires

For some, one group of rules has become the object of special reverence. Why such special feeling should be invested in these particular items is difficult to explain: They have probably become the symbolic flags around which those most intensely concerned with linguistic purity (whatever that may be) have tacitly agreed to rally. None of the items interferes with clarity and concision; indeed, some of them let us save a word here and there. But for one reason or another, they arouse such intense ire in so many editors, teachers, and ordinary citizens that you should be aware of their special status.

1.   Never use *like* for *as* or *as if.* Not this:

> These operations failed *like* the earlier ones did.
>
> It looks *like* we require further data on this matter.

But this:

> These operations failed *as* the earlier ones did.
>
> It looks *as if* we require further data on this matter.

2.   After *different,* use *from,* never *to* or *than.* Not this:

> These numbers are *different than* the ones you gave me earlier.
>
> We must approach this problem *differently than* we did last year.

But this:

> These numbers are *different from* the ones you gave me earlier.
>
> We must approach this problem *differently from the way* we did last year.

3. Use *hopefully* only when the subject of the sentence is in fact
    hopeful. Not this:

    Hopefully, the matter will be resolved soon.

But this:

    I hopefully say that the matter will be resolved soon.

4. Never qualify *unique* with a *very, rather, quite, somewhat,*
    etc. Not this:

    A *very unique* product was developed by his company.

5. Never use *finalize* to mean *finish, complete, end.*

6. Never use *irregardless* to mean *regardless.*

A Special Problem: Pronouns and Sexism

We expect verbs to agree with their subjects. Not this:

    There *is* several *reasons* for this.

But this:

    There *are* several *reasons* for this.

So do we ordinarily expect pronouns to agree in number with
what they refer to. Not this:

    The early *efforts* to oppose the building of a hydrogen bomb
    failed because *it* was not coordinated with the scientific and
    political communities. *No one* was willing to step forth and
    expose *themselves* to the anti-Communist hysteria unless
    they had the backing of others.

But this:

> The early *efforts* to oppose the building of a hydrogen bomb failed because *they* were not coordinated with the scientific and political communities. *No one* was willing to step forth and expose *himself* to the anti-Communist hysteria unless *he* had the backing of others.

There are two problems here. The first is whether to use a singular or plural noun when you refer to a singular noun that is plural in meaning: *group, committee, staff, administration* and so on. Some editors and teachers use a singular pronoun when the group acts as a single entity:

> The *committee* has reviewed the applications but has not yet made *its* decision.

But when the members of the group act individually, we always use a plural pronoun:

> The *committee* received the application, but not all of *them* have read it.

These days we find the plural used in both senses.

The second problem is what pronoun to use to refer to singular indefinite pronouns such as *everyone, everybody, someone, somebody,* and to indefinite singular nouns that refer to people but not to their gender: *a teacher, a person, a student,* and so on. In less formal writing, the plural *they* is being used increasingly.

> *Everyone* who spends four years in college realizes what a soft life *they* had only when *they* get a nine-to-five job, with no summer and Christmas vacations.

> When *a person* gets involved with drugs, no one can help *them* unless *they* want to help *themselves.*

In both cases, more formal usage requires the singular pronoun:

Everyone who spends four years in college realizes what a soft life *he* had only when *he* gets a nine-to-five job, with no summer and Christmas vacations.

When *a person* gets involved with drugs, no one can help *him* unless *he* wants to help *himself.*

But when we observe the formal rule, we raise another, thornier problem—the matter of sexist language.

Obviously, what we perceive to be our social responsibilities and the sensitivities of our audience must always come first: Many believe that we lose little, and gain much, by substituting *humankind* for *mankind, police officer* for *policeman, synthetic* for *man-made,* etc. (Those who ask whether we should also substitute *personhole cover* for *manhole cover,* or *person-in-the moon* for *man-in-the-moon,* either miss the point, or are making a contentious one.) And if we are writing for an audience that might judge our language sexist, then sheer common sense demands that we find ways to express our ideas in nonsexist ways, even at the cost of a little wordiness. We do little harm when we substitute for *The Dawn of Man* something like *The Dawn of Human Society.*

But a generic *he* is different: If we reject *he* as a generic pronoun because it is sexist, and *they* to refer to indefinite singulars because it is diffuse or potentially ambiguous (its formal "grammaticality" aside), we are left with either a clumsily intrusive *he or she* or an imperative to rewrite sentence after sentence in arbitrary and sometimes awkward ways.

Now, no one with even the dullest ear for style can choose the first alternative without flinching:

When a writer does not consider the ethnicity of his or her
readers, they may respond in ways he or she would not
have anticipated to certain words that for him or her are entirely innocent of ethnic bias.

So we have to rewrite. We can begin by substituting something for the singular *his,* perhaps plurals:

When a *writer* does not consider the ethnicity of *his* readers . . .

When *writers* do not consider the ethnicity of *their* readers . . .

We can also try passives, nominalizations, and other phrases that let us drop pronouns altogether:

> *Failure to consider* a reader's ethnic background may result in an *unexpected response* to certain words that the writer considers entirely innocent of ethnic bias.

And when it's appropriate, we can always try switching the pronoun from a third person *he* to a second person *you* or a first person *we:*

> If *we* do not consider the ethnic background of *our* readers, *they* may respond in ways *we* would not expect to certain words that to *us* are entirely innocent of ethnic bias.

Finally, each of us has to decide whether the social consequences of a sexist *he* justify the effort required to avoid it and the occasionally graceless or even diffuse style that that effort can produce. No one committed to writing the clearest, most fluent and precise prose can fail to recognize the value of a generic *he:* It lets us begin a sentence briskly and smoothly; it lets us assign to a verb specific agency; it lets us avoid ambiguity, diffuseness, and abstraction. But for the kind of practical writing that most of us do, fine nuances of phrasing and cadence may be less important than the social value of unqualified nonsexist language. Its cost is but a few moments' thought and an occasionally strained sentence; the cost is slight.

precision and PRECISION

You may assign some of the items taken up in this Lesson to categories different from those I have suggested. Some readers would add many other points of usage. And some would insist that every one of those items, and many more besides, belong in that first category, those constructions that invariably distinguish civilized speakers and writers of standard English from those who are not. If we don't respect all of these rules, they argue, we begin the slide down the slippery slope into national inarticulateness.

The impulse to regulate—and by regulating, fix—language has a long tradition, not only in the English-speaking world, but in literate cultures everywhere. We invest a great deal of ourselves first in learning our forms of speech, and then in mastering the fine points that, we are told, distinguish careful, responsible English from the language of those who are crude, careless, and unreliable. We believe that both our language and our values are threatened when we hear others use forms different from those we use, especially when those others seem to have values that threaten ours.

We usually express our linguistic values as a passionate concern for "precision," for maintaining "standards." Unless we maintain those standards, some argue, our language will degenerate into a barbarousness unequal to the needs of cultured discourse. But since no language has even been known to "degenerate" into a form that defeats effective communication, it is unlikely ours will.

We can put this matter of precision more usefully like this: If we ignore imprecise and clumsy writing, people will go on writing clumsily and imprecisely—in all the ways we've spent nine Lessons discussing. And if they go on writing clumsily and imprecisely, then eventually clumsiness and imprecision will become the accepted standard of written discourse. And when that happens, clumsy and imprecise thinking cannot be far behind. *That* is a matter worth some passion.

The trouble begins when we try to define the object of our passion, for, of course, we need examples of imprecise and clumsy writing that we can hold up for public abuse. But not many of us are going to memorize for this purpose good examples of bad writing (and even if we did, they would have no general use: Who writes the same sentence twice?). We find it much easier to assemble a list of stock items that we can cite as reliable examples of careless writing. When those items have been steadily abused for two and a half centuries, they become not just random items of disputed usage but symbols of the careful writer's dedication to the quality of his product. That's why, on TV talk shows and in newspapers and magazines, critics who deplore the declining state of the language always rehearse the same stock errors: *like* for *as, different than* for *different from, disinterested* for *uninterested, finalize, hopefully,* etc. These items have become the instantly recognized symbols of what we say we are fighting against in our determination to defend precise language. In fact, if tomorrow every writer of English began to observe every rule of usage, we should have to invent new ones, for their universal observance would substantially improve the language not at all and would deprive of their stock examples those for whom the purity of English is a special passion.

Most of us who are committed to excellence in prose share a common end: a style that communicates effectively, even elegantly when elegance is appropriate. And that, by and large, is a style that is clear, precise, and forceful. Some believe that we shall achieve that end only if we include in our definition of precision a precise adherence to all the rules of usage. Others do not. Wherever you decide to take your stand, keep this in mind: A writer who faithfully observes every one of these rules can still write wretched prose. And some of the most lucid, precise, and educated prose is written by those for whom *some* of these rules have no force whatsoever.

SUMMING UP
The Uses of Idiosyncracy

Because usage is largely a matter of personal taste—idiosyncratic, individual, unpredictable—I can offer no broad generalizations, no global principle by which to decide any given item. Indeed, if usage did submit to logical analysis and generalization, usage would be no issue, for most "errors" of usage result when a speaker or writer extends a regularity too far: When a speaker applies the past tense rule once too often, he produces the entirely logical *knowed*. The same impulse leads to other "errors:" *hisself* and *theirselves, ain't* as a perfectly logical and historically correct contraction of *am not, data* as a singular, since it lacks a plural—s. Indeed, the social utility of unpredictable rules is precisely in their idiosyncracy. It guarantees that only those with the leisure and inclination to learn them will do so.

Finally, I think, we choose among these items less on the

basis of their real or supposed correctness than according to a sense of our own personal style. Some of us are straightforward and plainspeaking; others take pleasure in a bit of elegance, of fastidiously self-conscious "class." The *shalls* and the *wills,* the *whos* and the *whoms,* the self-consciously unsplit infinitives—they are the small choices that let those of us who wish to do so, express that sense of linguistic conservatism that many believe testifies to their linguistic precision.

Style and Punctuation

I know there are some Persons who affect to despise it, and treat this whole Subject with the utmost Contempt, as a Trifle far below their Notice, and a Formality unworthy of their Regard: They do not hold it difficult, but despicable; and neglect it, as being above it.

Yet many learned Men have been highly sensible to its Use; and some ingenious and elegant Writers have condescended to point their Works with Care; and very eminent Scholars have not disdained to teach the Method of doing it with Propriety.

JAMES BURROW

In music, the punctuation is absolutely strict; the bars and rests are absolutely defined. But our prose cannot be quite strict, because we have to relate it to the audience. In other words we are continually changing the score.

SIR RALPH RICHARDSON

There are some punctuations that are interesting and there are some that are not.

GERTRUDE STEIN

For most of us, punctuation is a housekeeping problem: We engage it only long enough to keep things straight. And yet, deployed carefully and sensitively, commas, colons, and semi-colons can make our sentences* not only clear but even a bit stylish. Good punctuation won't turn a stylistic monotone into the Hallelujah Chorus, but a little knowledge and a bit of care can produce results that are quite gratifying.

Each section of this chapter begins with the least you have to know about punctuation and then explores some of its niceties. We'll address the matter as a functional problem: How do we punctuate the beginning, the middle, and the end of a sentence? And since how we punctuate the end of a sentence most visibly comments on our basic literacy, we'll begin there.

PUNCTUATING ENDS

In Lesson Six, we distinguished two kinds of sentences: *punctuated** and *grammatical**. A *punctuated sentence* is whatever begins with a capital letter and ends with a period, question mark, or exclamation point. A *grammatical sentence* is the least we can stop with one of those marks with nothing left over. The least a sentence can have is a finite verb*. And except for imperative sentences *(stop that!),* a grammatical sentence always provides that verb with a subject*. Together, the subject and verb constitute the spine of a clause*.

A clause is *independent** if it does not grammatically attach to, depend on, function as, a part of any other clause. You can punctuate an independent clause as a separate sentence.

> From 1925 to 1982, common stocks averaged an 8.5 percent return.

A *dependent* or *subordinate clause* usually begins with a word that signals its dependency: *because, although, if, since, when, though, after, before, as, which, who, whom, whose, that, whether.* We usually don't punctuate a dependent clause as a separate sentence. None of these:

> *Because* from 1925 to 1982, common stocks averaged an 8.5 percent return.

> *Which* from 1925 to 1982 averaged an 8.5 percent return.

> *That* from 1925 to 1982 common stocks averaged an 8.5 percent return.

Invariably, such a clause will attach to an independent clause that precedes or follows it:

> Common stocks would have been a good investment for more than the last half *century, because* from 1925 to 1982 they averaged an 8.5 percent return.

> You would have been wise to invest in common *stocks, which* from 1925 to 1982 averaged an 8.5 percent return.

> Few people are aware of this *fact, that* from 1925 to 1982 common stocks averaged an 8.5 percent return.

Another common kind of sentence fragment begins with *-ing*.

> Stocks have been a good investment. *Averaging* an 8.5 percent return from 1925 to 1982.

The phrase beginning with *averaging* has no subject, and *averaging* is not a form of a verb that could signal past or present. It would need an *are* or *were:*

> Stocks *were* averaging an 8.5 percent return from 1925 to 1982.

If we do not provide *averaging* with a subject and a finite verb, then we have to attach it to what goes before:

> Stocks have been a good *investment, averaging* an 8.5 percent. . . .

Joining Independent Clauses

Whenever you reach the end of a grammatical sentence, including whatever dependent clauses are part of it, you can stop with a period. But you can stop less emphatically in a few other ways: First, you can use a semicolon to indicate that your first independent clause is closely linked to a second independent clause that follows the semicolon:

> In 1957 and again in 1960, Congress passed civil rights laws that remedied problems of registration and *voting; both* had significant political consequences throughout the South.

> The Beatniks were the first identifiable postwar group to reject the values of the *middle-class; subsequent* years gave us Hippies, Yippies, flower children, dropouts, communards, and Weathermen.

Second, you can end one independent clause with a comma if the next clause is also a grammatical sentence and it begins with *and, but, yet, for, so, or,* or *nor:*

> In the 1950s religion came to be viewed as a bulwark against *communism, so it* was not long after that that atheism was felt to be a threat to national security.

> American intellectuals have always followed the lead of European Marxist *philosophy, but American* academic culture has proven to be an inhospitable environment for the flourishing of communistic ideas.

It is, of course, always considered absolutely wrong to run one independent clause onto the next with no connective at all:

> The stock market is finally beginning *to recover it was* depressed for several years.

If they are relatively short, closely linked, and balanced, you can link two grammatical sentences, two independent clauses, with just a comma: Be sure that neither has any internal commas.

> Football appeals to our love for *violence, baseball* satisfies our more measured and graceful tastes.

> Women have always been *underpaid, they* are only now beginning to do something about it.

Though it is not difficult to find sentences punctuated this way in the best prose, many teachers consider this kind of punctuation incorrect, so it is wise to have a sense of your audience before you experiment.

Nor is it uncommon for writers to join two short clauses with the conjunction alone, omitting the comma:

> Oscar Wilde brazenly violated one of the fundamental laws of British *society and we* all know what happened to him.

These four ways of linking clauses—(1) semicolon, (2) comma + coordinating conjunction, (3) comma alone, and (4) conjunction alone—create an increasingly tight bond between the ideas those clauses express, so it is important that the ideas in fact be closely connected.

Special Cases: Colon and Dash

A mark of punctuation that lets you be just the slightest bit elegant is the colon: It is formal shorthand for *to illustrate, for example, for instance, that is, let me expand on what I just said, therefore, the conclusion is obvious:*

> Only one question remains to be answered: Who assumes responsibility if the project loses money?

> Dance is not one of our more widely supported art forms: Not one dance company can count on operating in the black every year, and outside of two or three major cities, we find hardly any active companies.

> Computer operators are fond of comparing their hardware to the human brain: They wax eloquent on its speed, its resourcefulness, its flexibility.

A colon also lets you balance one clause against another a bit more elegantly than with a comma or semicolon:

> Civil disobedience is the public conscience of a democracy: Mass enthusiasm is the public consensus of a tyranny.

A dash can serve as a somewhat less formal colon—it has a kind of casual immediacy that suggests an afterthought:

> Stonehenge is one of the wonders of the ancient world—only a genius could have conceived, planned, and executed its mathematical and astronomical perfection.

(Try that with a colon—you'll sense the difference.)

You may or may not capitalize the first word in a clause following a colon: A capital letter makes what follows a bit more prominent and emphatic. Ordinarily, we don't capitalize what follows a dash.

Avoid putting a colon between a verb and a long object. Not this:

> Effective genetic counseling *requires*: *a thorough* knowledge of statistical genetics, an awareness of medical choices open to prospective parents, psychological competence to deal with emotional trauma.

Complete the clause before you begin a substantial list:

> Effective genetic counseling requires the following *preparation*: *a thorough knowledge* of statistical genetics, an awareness of . . . .

PUNCTUATING BEGINNINGS

If you begin a sentence directly with a subject, you have no problems. Problems begin when you introduce a sentence with modifying words, phrases, and clauses. You can follow a few absolute rules, but more often you have to exercise good judgment.

The (almost) Absolute Rules

1. Never put a comma after an introductory subordinating conjunction such as *because, if, although, while, since, as, before, after.* Not this:

    > *Because, inflation* is increasing faster than interest rates, people are investing their money in art objects.

2. Resist a comma after the introductory coordinating conjunctions *and, but, yet, for, so, or, nor*. Not this:

> *But, we* cannot know whether life on other planets realizes that we're here and simply prefers to ignore us.

> *And, this* conclusion supports that of earlier research.

Some writers who punctuate heavily will put a comma after *and, but, yet, for, so, or, nor* if an introductory word or phrase follows:

> *Yet, during this period, prices* continued to rise.

That is a matter of taste.

3. Generally put a comma after introductory words or phrases such as *however, nevertheless, regardless, instead, on the other hand, as a result, consequently, moreover, furthermore, that is, also, fortunately, obviously, allegedly, incidentally*—any word or phrase that comments on the whole of the following sentence:

> *Furthermore, psychological* studies indicate that student radicals are no more neurotic or disturbed than others.

If you find yourself introducing sentence after sentence with words like these, you might consider revising a bit. A comma after just a word or two slows the pace of a sentence just when it should be gaining momentum. Too many such sentences retard the flow of the whole passage.

Four introductory words often appear without a following comma: *now, therefore, thus, hence:*

> *Now it* is clear that many constituencies will not support this position.

> *Thus the* only alternative is to choose some other action.

4. Always separate an introductory word, phrase, or clause—no matter how short—from what follows if a reader might misunderstand:

When the lawyer concludes the opening statement from the floor may begin.

In most cases we have treated these conditions over a period of several years.

If you open a sentence with a short introductory phrase before a short subject, you don't need a comma:

Once again we find similar responses to exodermal stimuli.

In 1945 few returning servicemen anticipated the dramatic social changes that had transformed American society.

In many areas of the country gasoline prices have risen twice as fast as food prices.

It's not an error to use a comma after an introductory phrase, but contemporary writers tend to use less punctuation than even those of the recent past.

Close Connections

With introductory subordinate clauses, there are some other considerations: How closely does the meaning of the introductory clause relate to the meaning of the main clause? If you open with a subordinate clause whose subject is the same as the subject of the main clause, and the meaning of one clause closely depends on the meaning of the other, you probably won't need a comma:

When Hitler realized his Eastern front had collapsed he resolved to destroy every city through which his army would retreat.

But if the subjects of the two clauses differ and the ideas contrast, then you probably do need a comma. Compare:

Because *we* have accepted the interpretation of the *IRS we* will drop all further appeals.

Although *the IRS* has overruled this *interpretation, we* will continue to follow our original procedures.

Semicolons have no place between an introductory element and a subject, so you can forget about using them there. But if your subject is a long list, then try a colon or a dash followed by a summative subject.

Compare:

The President, the Vice-President, the Secretaries of the Executive Departments, the Supreme Court Justices, Senators, and members of the House of Representatives take an oath of office that pledges them to uphold the Constitution.

The President, the Vice-President, the Secretaries of the Executive Departments, the Supreme Court Justices, Senators, and members of the House of Representatives: *all* take an oath of office that pledges them to uphold the Constitution.

Drugs, gambling, violence, poverty, disease, despair constitute a familiar list of afflictions that destroy the fabric of a community.

Drugs, gambling, violence, poverty, disease, despair—*they* constitute a familiar list of afflictions that destroy the fabric of a community.

Whether you choose the dash or the colon depends mostly on how formal you want to be.

PUNCTUATING THE MIDDLE

Explaining how to punctuate inside a sentence, clause, or phrase is messy, because we have to consider combinations of grammar, meaning, and rhythm. There are, though, three principles to follow:

1. Set off with commas or dashes that which distinctly interrupts.
2. Set off with commas, dashes, or parentheses that which loosely comments on or explains essential parts of a clause or phrase.
3. Separate with commas or semicolons items in a series of three or more.

Interruptions

When you insert any kind of phrase or clause between a subject and its verb, you usually have to set off that interruption with commas:

> Religious education, *I repeat,* is an affair of the private conscience, not of the body politic.

> The history of every animal species, *regardless of its evolutionary status,* proves that the most adaptive survive the longest.

> This one principle of TV programming, *because it simply overpowers all other considerations,* determines what each of us will watch morning, noon, and night.

(Better yet—avoid the interruptions. Move the interrupter.)

Adverbs* or phrases inside a verb phrase* take commas or not, depending on what your ear prefers:

> Twentieth-century poetry *has in recent years become* more comprehensible to the average reader.

> Twentieth-century poetry *has, in recent years, become* more comprehensible to the average reader.

It depends entirely on how emphatic you want to be.

If you separate a verb and its object with a phrase or word that is shorter than the object, you don't have to set it off with commas:

> In moments of great anxiety, we *see perhaps too clearly the stuff* of which our characters are made.

But if the object is considerably shorter and you want to arrange the words for the greatest impact, you might set off the interruption with a comma:

> The antagonisms between the scientific and humanistic communities have created, *in virtually every quarter of the scholarly and intellectual world,* utter distrust.

Loose Commentary

What counts as "loose commentary" depends on meaning, not on grammar. The usual distinction is between *restrictive** and *nonrestrictive** modifiers. A nonrestrictive modifier is "loose"; it adds information to describe something that has already been identified sufficiently.

Compare these:

It was necessary partly to reconstruct the larynx, *which had received a traumatic injury,* by means of cartilage obtained from the shoulder.

Tax deduction dependency is awarded to the *parent with whom the child principally resides.*

Since we have only one larynx, merely naming it identifies it sufficiently. Anything more we say about it is loose, *nonrestrictive, nonspecifying* commentary, and so we set it off with commas. But since children have two parents, simply referring to one of them as *parent* doesn't identify which parent we mean. So to *parent* we add a *restrictive,* specifying modifier to identify *which* parent we mean. And in that case, we *don't* set off the modifier with commas.

Phrases and clauses that conclude a sentence should be preceded by a comma unless they are essential to the meaning of the main clause. Compare these:

Hemingway wandered through Europe, *seeking some environment where he could write what he felt he had to.*

Hemingway spent *most of his time seeking some environment where he could write what he felt he had to.*

All offices will be closed from July 2 through July 6, *as announced in the daily bulletin.*

When closing the offices, it is important *to secure all desks and safes as prescribed in Operating Manual 45-23a.*

Those who describe what a technologically spendid future we have to look forward to usually underestimate the effect of seemingly minor *social changes, at least insofar as this country is concerned.*

These records must *be maintained at least until the IRS has decided whether to review them.*

But, again, this is often settled by a good ear rather than a fixed rule.

In some of these cases, a dash is more casual—or striking—than a comma:

> The process was repeated a fourth time—*successfully.*

> It was necessary to fix up his voice box—*which really got hit hard*—by taking some cartilage from his shoulder.

A dash is particularly useful when the chunk of "loose commentary" has internal commas. This is just a bit confusing:

> All the nations of Central Europe, Poland, Czechoslovakia, Hungary, Roumania, Bulgaria, and Yugoslavia, have known what it is like to be in the middle of an East-West tug-of-war.

But if we set off that middle chunk with dashes, the sentence is much clearer:

> All the nations of Central Europe—Poland, Czechoslovakia, Hungary, Roumania, Bulgaria, and Yugoslavia—have known what it is like to be in the middle of an East-West tug-of-war.

Parentheses serve much the same function, though they are usually more appropriate when you want to suggest that you are inserting a kind of *sotto voce* aside:

> The brain (if our theories are correct) is really two brains operating simultaneously.

Or explanatory information:

> Lamarck (1744-1829) was a French naturalist and pre-Darwinian evolutionist.

> The poetry of the *fin de siècle* (end of the century) period was characterized by a world-weariness and fashionable despair that was closer to intellectual vapidity than spiritual emptiness.

Series

The least complicated punctuation is that of the series. Once you decide whether or not to use a comma before the *and,* you don't have too many more decisions:

> His wit, his charm, and his appearance made him everyone's friend.

> His wit, his *charm and* his appearance made him everyone's favorite.

Whichever you choose, be consistent. The advantage in always putting the comma before *and* is that you'll never confuse a reader about whether the last two items are supposed to be taken as a unit or separately:

> The Treasurer will issue separate reports on the yields for Treasury notes, grain futures, common *stocks and bonds.*

If any of the items in the series needs internal commas, then use semicolons to set off the items:

> In mystery novels, the principal action ought to be economical, organic, and logical; fascinating, yet not exotic; clear but complicated enough to hold the reader's interest—a compromise that is not always easy to strike.

How you punctuate a series of adjectives before a noun depends on whether you intend them to be rhetorically equal or increasingly specific:

> Everyone likes a big red juicy apple.

> We shall eliminate all nonfunctioning, nonrepairable, obsolete units.

Big is more general than *red, red* more general than *juicy,* so we put them in that order without commas. Compare: *a juicy red big apple.* But *nonfunctioning, nonrepairable,* and *obsolete* are equally specific, so we coordinate them with commas. Compare: *an obsolete, nonrepairable, nonfunctioning unit,* a phrase just as acceptable as the original.

Punctuating Coordinate Elements

Ordinarily, don't put a comma between coordinated words and phrases:

> As computers have become more sophisticated, *and more powerful*, they have taken over more *clerical, and bookkeeping* tasks.

> As computers have become more *sophisticated and more powerful,* they have taken over more *clerical and bookkeeping* tasks.

There are, however, some exceptions:

1. If you want a more intense effect, drop out the *and* and insert a comma.

    Compare:

    > Abraham Lincoln never had the advantage of *a formal education and never owned* a large library.

    > Abraham Lincoln never had the advantage of *a formal education, never owned* a large library.

    > The great lesson of the pioneers was to stop complaining about conditions that seem difficult or *even overwhelming and to get on* with the business of shaping a life in a hostile environment.

    > The great lesson of the pioneers was to stop complaining about conditions that seem difficult or even overwhelming, *to get on with* the business of shaping a life in a hostile environment.

2. A long coordinate pair occasionally needs a comma to interrupt what otherwise would be a monotonous flow:

    > It is in the graveyard scene that Hamlet finally realizes that the inevitable end of all life is the *grave and that regardless* of one's station in life the end of all pretentiousness and all plotting and counterplotting must be clay.

    > It is in the graveyard scene that Hamlet finally realizes that the inevitable end of all life is the *grave, and that regardless* of one's station in life, the end of all pretentiousness and all plotting and counterplotting must be clay.

3. Sometimes we put a comma even after a short coordinate element if we want a dramatic pause:

These conclusions are rather *thin, and even incaccurate.*

The ocean is one of nature's most glorious *creations, and one of its most destructive.*

This is especially common before a *but:*

Organ transplants are becoming increasingly *common, but* not less expensive.

4. And finally, we can put a comma after a short or long coordinate element if its absence might mislead our reader about the grammar of a sentence:

Conrad's *Heart of Darkness* inquires into those primitive impulses that lie deep in each of us and stir only in our darkest dreams and asserts the unassailable need for the civilized values and institutions that control those impulses.

A comma after *dreams* would clearly mark the end of one coordinate member and the beginning of the next:

Conrad's *Heart of Darkness* inquires into those primitive impulses that lie deep in each of us and stir only in our darkest *dreams, and asserts* the unassailable need for the civilized values and institutions that control those impulses.

Exercise 10–1

Here are two passages minus all their original punctuation. Extra spacings   indicate boundaries of grammatical sentences. Punctuate these passages twice, once using the least punctuation possible, then a second time using as much varied punctuation as you can. Then do it a third time in the way that you think most effective.

1. From all available evidence no black man had ever set foot in this tiny Swiss village before I came   I was told before arriving that I would probably be a "sight" for the village   I took this to mean that people of my complexion were rarely seen in Switzerland and also that people are always something of a

"sight" outside the city   it did not occur to me possibly because I am an American that there could be people anywhere who had never seen a Negro   it is a fact that cannot be explained on the basis of the   inaccessibility of the village   the village is very high   but it is only four hours from Milan and three hours from Lausanne   it is true that it is virtually unknown   few people making plans for a holiday would elect to come here   on the other hand the villagers are able presumably to come and go as they please which they do to another town at the foot of the mountain with a population of approximately five thousand the nearest place to see a movie or go to the bank   in the village there is no movie house no bank no library no theater very few radios one jeep one station wagon and at the moment one typewriter mine an invention which the woman next door to me here had never seen   there are about six hundred people living here all Catholic   I conclude this from the fact that the Catholic church is open all year round whereas the Protestant chapel set off on a hill a little removed from the village is open only in the summertime when the tourists arrive   there are four or five hotels all closed now and four or five bistros of which however only two do any business during the winter   these two do not do a great deal   for life in the village seems to end around nine or ten o'clock   there are a few stores butcher baker *épicerie,* a hardware store and a moneychanger who cannot change travelers' checks but must send them down to the bank an operation which takes two or three days   there is something called the Ballet Hall closed in the winter and used for God knows what certainly not ballet in the summer   there seems to be only one schoolhouse in the village and this for the quite young children

—James Baldwin, "Stranger in the Village," from *Notes of a Native Son*

2. In fact of course the notion of universal knowledge has always been an illusion   but it is an illusion fostered by the monistic view of the world in which a few great central truths determine in all its wonderful and amazing proliferation everything else that is true   we are not today tempted to search for these keys that unlock the whole of human knowledge and of man's experience   we know that we are ignorant   we are well taught it   and the more surely and

deeply we know our own job the better able we are to appreciate the full measure of our pervasive ignorance   we know that these are inherent limits compounded no doubt and exaggerated by that sloth and that complacency without which we would not be men at all   but knowledge rests on knowledge   what is new is meaningful because it departs slightly from what was known before   this is a world of frontiers where even the liveliest of actors or observers will be absent most of the time from most of them   perhaps this sense was not so sharp in the village that village which we have learned a little about but probably do not understand too well the village of slow change and isolation and fixed culture which evokes our nostalgia even if not our full comprehension   perhaps in the villages men were not so lonely   perhaps they found in each other a fixed community a fixed and only slowly growing store of knowledge of a single world   even that we may doubt   for there seem to be always in the culture of such times and places vast domains of mystery if not unknowable then imperfectly known endless and open

> —J. Robert Oppenheimer, "The Sciences and Man's Community," from *Science and the Common Understanding*

SUMMING UP
Reasonable Punctuation

1. At the end of a grammatical sentence, use one of the following.
    a. A period, question mark, or exclamation point, even if the next sentence begins with *and, but, yet, for, so, or, nor:*

    At first, the group was strangely unresponsive. *But* as the meeting progressed, they became more animated.

    b. A semicolon, if the next grammatical sentence does not begin with *and, but, yet, for, so, or, nor:*

Imagination is not a literary gift; *it* is part of being a human being.

c.   A comma, if the next grammatical sentence begins with *and, but, yet, for, so, or, nor:*

It is true, as Marshall McLuhan says, that the medium is the message, *but* it is also true that the message is considerably more than just the medium.

But if the first grammatical sentence has a good deal of internal punctuation, use a semicolon before the conjunction:

In the sciences, new facts, new theories, are not merely added to the sum of knowledge, regardless of how long and how established that sum of knowledge might be; *nor do* those new facts and new theories merely replace the old, as a new brick completely fills the space of one that has been removed and discarded.

d.   A colon if what follows the colon is a list, or a restatement, consequence, conclusion, or illustration of the first sentence:

Harry Truman entered office as one of the least promising of our presidents: *He* had been a minor senator from Missouri, an obedient political partyman, and someone who Roosevelt believed would best serve his country by presiding over the Senate, quietly.

e.   Just a comma if the grammatical sentences are short, do not contain internal punctuation, and are closely related and rhetorically balanced:

I came, *I* saw, *I* went away impressed.

f.   Just an *and, but, yet, so, for, or, nor* if the grammatical sentences are short and balanced:

American fisherman argued for a 200-mile limit *and the American public* supported them.

More tried to turn Einstein into a political pundit *but he* would have none of it.

Compare:

> Texas and Louisiana have requested that Mexico pay for the recent oil spill that polluted their coasts and damaged their fishing and tourist industry, *but Mexico* has flatly refused.

> No public official has the right to set him- or herself above the law, *and it's* clear that the American public is not about to change that principle.

    g.   A dash, if the following grammatical sentence is short and dramatic:

> We are all a product of our environment—so why do we abuse it?

2.   In the beginning of a grammatical sentence, use the following punctuation:
    a.   Nothing after conjunctions such as *because, if, when, after, although, unless, before, since, as.* Not:

> Academic freedom is the foundation of a free society *because, it* prevents the state from using the educational system for its own ends.

    b.   Nothing after *and, but, yet, for, so, nor, or.* Not:

> Both Kennedy and Nixon were qualified to be President in 1960. *But, Kennedy* knew how to manipulate the media more effectively.

    c.   A comma after a word or phrase that relates to the whole of the following sentence:

> *Therefore,* to appreciate ballet is to appreciate both animal grace and the grace of intellect.

    d.   A comma if your reader can mistake the grammar of a sentence. Not:

> If you want to improve , your mind and your soul must be disciplined.

e. A comma after a long (more than six or so words) introductory element:

Regardless of any appearance of random or even accidental form, a work of modern art always implies a deliberate intention.

f. A dash or a colon between a subject consisting of a list and a word that summarizes the list:

Copernicus, Galileo, Newton, Darwin, Freud, Einstein—they did not give us new and unfamiliar things to look at so much as new ways to look at familiar things.

The freedom to travel, to worship, to read what we will, to gather and discuss the conduct of our lives: Such privileges are unknown in most of the world.

3. Inside a sentence, punctuate as follows:
a. Set off obvious interruptions with commas or dashes:

The women's movement—*I use the term loosely and inclusively*—has brought together many women who otherwise never would have met.

A nation, *they say,* gets the government it deserves.

b. Set off parenthetical, nonrestrictive, loosely added material with commas, with parentheses (infrequently), or with dashes (even more infrequently):

Toscanini, *who assuredly will be remembered as the premier maestro of the twentieth century,* never exaggerated his own abilities.

During this period (*from roughly the middle of June to the end of summer*), Allied forces advanced very slowly.

Every ruler—*king, president, prime minister, or tyrant*—surrounds himself with advisers who will assure him he is always right.

c. Separate items in a list with commas, or if those items are themselves punctuated with commas, with semicolons:

This will require *money, effort, and* time.

I shall first discuss Hamlet, a tragedy of the intellect; then Lear, a tragedy of the heart; and finally Macbeth, a tragedy of the soul.

4. Separate two coordinated items with a comma under the following conditions.

    a. When the beginning of the second element can be mistaken for a continuation of the first:

We must continue to believe that we can shape our future and achieve our goal, and resolutely dedicate ourselves to that effort.

    b. When the first item is so long that its rhythm becomes monotonous:

Myths constitute the record of those prehistorical events that have given shape to a preliterate culture, and give dramatic power to the cultural values that hold that shape.

    c. When you want to give the second element a dramatic turn:

We must never underestimate the power of an aroused citizenry, or overestimate it.

Some Terms Defined

There is a satisfactory boniness about grammar which the flesh of sheer vocabulary requires before it can become vertebrate and walk the earth. But to study it for its own sake, without relating it to function, is utter madness.

ANTHONY BURGESS

Thou hast most traitorously corrupted the youth of the realm in erecting a grammar school. . . . It will be proved to thy face that thou hast men about thee that usually talk of a noun and a verb, and such abominable words as no Christian ear can endure to hear.

WILLIAM SHAKESPEARE, 2 *HENRY VI*, 4.7

What follows does not reflect a tightly systematic theory of grammar. It is merely reliable advice about how to understand the terms starred in the text, *for the purposes of this text,* and how to identify examples of what they refer to. Each definition has its exceptions, but each remains serviceable for the study of style.

Action: For our purposes, a very broad concept. It includes all movement, feeling, cogitation, creation, attention, condition, etc. Typically, an action is expressed by a verb*: *move, hate, think, discover, watch.* But it may be expressed as a noun*: *movement, hatred, thought, discovery.* Conditions are typically expressed by adjectives*: *careful, intelligent, large, transparent;* but these, too, may be expressed by nouns: *carefulness, intelligence, largeness, transparency.* Some actions may be expressed only by nouns: *motion, transition, contempt.*

Active: An active verb* usually (not always) has the doer of its action* as its subject* and never occurs in its past participle* form after a form of *be.* It may occur in its past participle form after *have:*

> I have *checked* the results.

It may occur after *be* if the verb is in its present participle* form:

> I am *checking* the results.

A passive* verb always has as its subject* that toward which an action is directed. It always occurs in its past participle form after a form of *be* (or *get):*

> The results have *been checked.*
> The results are *being checked.*

Adjective: An adjective qualifies or limits a noun. You can identify adjectives by putting a *very* in front of a word you think might be one: *very old, very intelligent, very interesting, very fascinated.* There are a few words we might want to call adjectives that this test will not identify: *major, additional, resumptive, occupational,* etc. You can identify such words as adjectives by trying them out between *the* and an appropriate noun: *The* **occupational** *hazard, the* **major** *reason, an* **additional** *problem,* etc. Unfortunately, because some nouns occur in the same place: *the* **chemical** *hazard,* this method is not always reliable.

Adjective Phrase: An adjective* and whatever attaches to it:

> *so* **large** *that no one could carry it*

Adverb: This term refers to a potpourri of items. Adverbs are words that modify parts of speech other than nouns*. Adverbs can modify

> Adjectives*: ***extremely** large, **rather** old, **very** tired*
>
> Verbs*: ***frequently** spoke, **often** slept, left **here***
>
> Adverbs: ***very** carefully, **somewhat** often, **a bit** late*
>
> Articles*: ***precisely** the man I meant, **just** the thing we need*
>
> Whole sentences*: ***Fortunately,** we were on time;* **consequently,** *we saw the show.*

Adverb Phrase: The adverb* and whatever attaches to it:

> *too*   **carefully**   *to be accidental*

Agent: The originating force of an action*, the source of an action, the responsible party, that entity without which an action could not occur.

Article: *a, the, this, that, these, those.*

Clause: Except for imperatives *(Come here!),* a clause has a subject* and a verb* that can be in a past or present form (it's called a finite* verb: *goes, went;* as opposed to an infinitive* verb: *to go).* These are all clauses:

He left.	Why he left
Because he left	That he left

By this definition, *for him to leave* is not a clause, because the verb *leave* is in its infinitive* form, not in its finite form; nor is *his examining the document* a clause, because *examining* cannot be turned into *examined:*

There are two kinds of clauses: *subordinate* and *main* (or independent). Subordinate clauses usually begin with some kind of subordinating conjunction*.

Adverbial subordinate clauses comment on time, cause, condition, etc. They usually begin with subordinating conjunctions such as *because, although, when, if, since, before, as, after, while, unless:*

> **Unless** *you leave,* I will take action.
>
> **Because** *you have not left,* I've called the police.
>
> **When** *you leave,* close the door.

Adjectival* subordinate clauses describe nouns*. They are also called relative* clauses and usually begin with the relative pronouns *which, that, whom, whose, who:*

> The book **that** *I bought for you* was expensive.
>
> My car, **which** *you just saw,* is gone.
>
> A woman **whose** *aunt lives down the street* just called.

We can identify two kinds of relative clauses: restrictive (also called "defining,") and nonrestrictive. A nonrestrictive clause is a clause that is not necessary to identify the noun* phrase it modifies. We ordinarily set such a phrase off with commas as a kind of parenthetical addition. A restrictive clause, on the other hand, uniquely identifies the noun it modifies, and ordinarily we do not set such a phrase off with commas because the clause is not parenthetical but necessary. For example, since a person has only one birthday, no modifying phrase can make the phrase *my birthday* any more specific than it already is. So we would set off anything we say about a birthday with commas:

> My birthday, **which I keep a secret,** was last month.

This would make no sense:

My birthday **which I keep a secret** was last month.

We would be suggesting that we had more than one birthday, one that we keep secret and at least one other that we don't.

On the other hand, a restrictive clause is a modifying clause that identifies one from among many. For example, if we began to write about friends and wanted to distinguish among them, we would ordinarily require a restrictive clause:

My friends **who live in Ohio** write me every month.

Once we have identified our friends, however, we would use a nonrestrictive clause, since our reader would know to whom we were referring.

These friends, **who in fact know you,** will visit soon.

For a discussion of whether to use *that* or *which* in these contexts, see p. 179.
  Subordinate clauses that function like nouns usually begin with subordinating conjunctions such as *that, what, why, how, who, when, where, whether:*

I don't know *what I should do.*

That she is not here worries me.

I'll ask *whether we can stay.*

I already told you *who came.*

  There are exceptions to all three cases. In this next sentence, the three subordinate clauses are introduced by an adverbial *if,* a relative *which,* and a subordinating conjunction, *that:*

If we had the resources which you have described, I don't doubt *that we could do better.*

But we can omit them:

[   ] *Had we the resources* [   ] *you have described,* I don't doubt
[   ] *we could do better.*

Main, or independent clauses have their own subjects and
finite verbs and do not function as adjectives, adverbs, or nouns.

Complement: A complement completes a verb* that needs completing, that is unfinished without something following it (including direct objects*):

	Verb	**Complement**
I	am	*in the house.*
We	seem	*tired.*
She	discovered	*the money.*
He	began	*to do the job.*

Compound Noun: You can't tell from spelling alone when a
pair of words is a compound noun. Some are separate words:
space capsule, retirement home, police station; some are
hyphenated: *mother-in-law, eighty-two;* some are written as one
word: *beehive, airport, bookkeeper.* A reliable test is pronunciation: If the first word is stressed more than the second, the word is
a compound word: *dóg hòuse, spáce càpsule, bóok dèaler.* On the
other hand, some phrases that seem to be compounds are stressed
on the second word: *gàrden páth, stòne wáll, fàther cónfessor.*

Conjunction: Usually defined as a word that links two other
words, phrases*, or clauses*. But verbs* and prepositions* do the
same thing. It's easier to illustrate conjunctions than to define
them precisely.

Adverbial conjunctions: *because, although, when, since, if, unless,
while, after,* etc.

(See *adverbial clause* under Clause*.)

Relative conjunction or relative pronoun: *who, whom, whose,
which, that*

(See *relative clause* under Clause*.)

Sentence conjunction: *thus, however, therefore, consequently,
nevertheless, on the other hand, in fact,* etc.

Coordinating conjunction: *and, but, yet, for, so, or, nor*

(See Coordination*.)

Correlative coordinating* conjunctions: *both X and Y,*
not only X but also Y,
either X or Y, neither X
nor Y, X as well as Y

Coordination: We coordinate grammatically equal elements:

Words: *you **and** me, red **and** black, run **or** jump, old **yet** strong*

Phrases: *in the house **but** not in the basement, very young **and***
very smart

Clauses*: *when I leave **or** when you arrive*

Ordinarily, the coordinated phrases and clauses have to be of the same grammatical order:

Not: *for him to leave **and** that she stayed*

But: *that he left **and** that she stayed*

Or: *for him to leave **and** for her to stay*

Correlative Conjunction: See Conjunction.* Ordinarily, both members of a pair of correlative conjunctions should introduce a word, phrase, or clause with the same form:

Not: He ***both** had the data **and** the equipment* to display it.

But: He had ***both** the data **and** the equipment* to display it.

Not: The shipment will ***either** arrive on Monday **or** on Wednes-*
day.

But: The shipment will arrive ***either** on Monday **or** on Wednesday.*

Or: The shipment will arrive on ***either** Monday **or** Wednesday.*

Direct Object: See Object*.

Finite Verb: See Verb*.

Free Modifier: A phrase added to the end of a clause that modifies the subject of the clause:

> She walked down the street, *ready for anything.* (i.e., she was ready . . .)
>
> I tried to explain the problem, *pointing out all the difficulties.* (i.e., I pointed out . . .)
>
> The fire engine appeared, *siren screaming.* (i.e., The fire engine had a siren . . .)

We call it "free" because usually it can also go before the subject:

> *Ready for anything,* she walked down the street.

Goal: That toward which an action* seems to be directed. It may be that which is affected, created, observed, perceived, changed, etc. In most cases, goals are expressed as direct objects*: In some cases, the goal can be the subject of an active* verb*:

I see you	I underwent an interrogation.
I broke the dish	She received a
I built a house	warm welcome.

Grammatical Sentence: A sentence that cannot be separated by a period into two sentences that without further change could stand by themselves. Traditional grammarians call sentences either *simple* or *complex:*

> Simple: *The bureau* in London *is* no longer responsible for overseas planning, making it a less influential office.
>
> Complex: *The bureau* in London *is* no longer responsible for overseas planning, [because *we have* centralized operations].

Neither of these can be broken into two sentences with a period.

When a single punctuated sentence contains more than one grammatical sentence, traditional grammarians call it a *compound sentence* if each of the grammatical sentences consists of a single main clause*:

Cleveland won, and Washington lost.

If the punctuated sentence contains two main clauses and one or more subordinate clauses* then traditional grammarians call it a *compound-complex* sentence:

We stayed because we had paid in advance, but they left.

We can change the first example to two simple sentences and the second to a complex and a simple sentence merely by separating them with periods before *and* and *but*.

Cleveland won. And Washington Lost.

We stayed because we had paid in advance. But they left.

The difference between traditional terminology and the terminology I have used here is important: When we talk about "long" sentences, we may have to distinguish a long punctuated sentence from a long grammatical sentence. When a long punctuated sentence consists of several grammatical sentences (compound or compound-complex in the terminology of traditional grammar), a reader can usually follow it much more easily than he can a long punctuated sentence made up of a single grammatical sentence.

Independent Clause: See Clause*.

Infinitive: See Verb*.

Inflection: See Verb*, inflected.

Intransitive Verb: A kind of verb* that does not take an object* and cannot be made into a passive* verb. These are not transitive* verbs:

He *exists*. They *left* town. She *became* a queen.

Linking Verb: A verb whose complement* modifies or refers to the same thing as its subject*.

Linking: He *is* my brother. She *seems* reliable. They *became* teachers. It *appears* broken.

Main Clause: See Clause*.

Metadiscourse: Writing about writing, whatever does not refer to the subject matter being addressed. This includes all connecting devices such as *therefore, however, for example, in the first place;* all comment about the author's attitude: *I believe, in my opinion, let me also point out;* all comment about the writer's confidence in his following assertion: *most people believe, it is widely assumed, allegedly;* references to the audience: *as you can see, you will find that, consider now the problem of.* . . .

Nominalization: A noun* based on, derived from, communicating the same information as a verb* or adjective*: *move-movement, act-action; resist-resistance, good-goodness, intelligent-intelligence, elastic-elasticity.*

Nonrestrictive Clause: See Clause*.

Noun: A word that will fit into the following position: The _____ is good.

Object: There are three kinds of objects: (1) prepositional object; the noun* that follows a preposition* *(in the house, by the walk, across the street, with fervor);* (2) direct object: the noun that follows a transitive verb* (I *read the book,* we *followed the car);* (3) indirect object: a noun or pronoun directly after a verb, preceding a direct object. The same noun or pronoun can also appear as the object of a preposition following a direct object:

I gave *my friend* a book.

I gave   a book *to my friend.*

He bought *me* some flowers.

He bought   some flowers *for me.*

Orienter: A word or phrase, usually occurring at the beginning of a sentence* or clause*, that (1) sets what follows in a time or place, (2) gives the reader a point of view toward what follows, or (3) provides some other context that allows a reader to understand an assertion correctly:

> *In the morning,* insects are relatively inactive.
>
> *Politically speaking,* the Old Left has little influence anymore.
>
> *Under most circumstances,* mammals will fight to protect their young.

Passive: See Active*.

Past Participle: Most verbs signal past participle forms with *-ed; walked, jumped; worked, investigated.* Irregular verbs have irregular past participle forms: *seen, broken, swum, stolen, hurt, been,* etc. When they follow a *have,* they are in their "perfect" form:

> I *have* **gone.** Her friends *have* **arrived.** We *had* **been** there.

Past participle forms also function as modifiers:

> a *broken* arm, a *twisted* leg, a *scratched* face.

Phrase: A group of words that constitute a unit but do not comprise a subject* and a finite verb*. There are noun phrases, which center on a noun* and may include modifying elements: *the little* **book** *on the table;* verb phrases: *may have been found;* and adjective* and adverb* phrases.

Predicate: Roughly, whatever follows the subject*. *He* **went** **downtown yesterday to buy a suit.** Whatever introduces a sentence that could appear with the predicate is also part of the predicate: **Yesterday,** *he* **went downtown.**

Preposition: Roughly, like conjunctions,* prepositions are easier to list than to define: *in, on, up, over, out, under, between, at, toward, with, by, across,* etc.

Prepositional Phrase: The preposition* plus its noun* object*: *in the house, by the door, without enthusiasm.*

Present Participle: The *-ing* form of the verb. It can be used as the *progressive* form of the verb (always following a form of *be):*

> He was *running.* I am *listening.* You *are going.*

Or as a modifier:

> *Running* streams are beautiful. *Working* wives are common.

Or as the *gerundive* form, the form that functions as a noun:

> *Running* is good for you. *Listening* is important.

Some consider this gerundive *-ing* to be different from the participial *-ing.* They are probably right.

Progressive: See Verb*.

Punctuated Sentence: Whatever begins with a capital letter and ends with a period, question mark, or exclamation point.

Relative Clause: See Clause*.

Relative Pronoun: See Clause*.

Restrictive Clause: See Clause*.

Resumptive Modifier: A resumptive modifier is added to the end of a phrase or clause. It repeats a word used at or near the end of that phrase or clause.

> East Coast columnists and commentators delight in expressing their own narrow **view** of the world,
> > *a view . . .*

To this repeated word is added more information:

> . . . own narrow ***view*** of the world, ***a view shaped by the insular and heated intellectualism that characterizes the East Coast liberal establishment.***

Sentence: There is no easy way to define a *sentence* that would be useful here. It's useful to distinguish two kinds, however: grammatical sentence* and punctuated sentence*.

Stress: The end of a sentence*, what should be the location of the ideas that you want to emphasize or that you will expand on in the next sentence.

Subject: The subject is whatever the verb* agrees with in person and number:

> *Two men are* at the door.

> *One man is* at the door.

We can see that *there* in

> There *was a man* at the door.

> There *were two men* at the door.

is the subject of neither sentence. It is merely a function word that fills the slot that we expect before a verb.

You can always identify a subject once you have identified the verb: Simply put a *who* or a *what* in front of the verb and turn the sentence into a question. The answer to the question is the subject of the sentence:

> That ontogeny recapitulates phylogeny *is* an accepted evolutionary fact.

> Question: *What is* an accepted evolutionary fact?

> Answer (and subject): That ontogeny recapitulates phylogeny.

(This doesn't work with sentences beginning with *there.)*

Subordinate Clause: See Clause*.

Subordinating Conjunction: *Because, if, when, since, although,* etc.

Summative Modifier: A summative modifier occurs at the end of a clause. It begins by summing up the clause:

> Few economists believe the price of gold will go to $1,000 an ounce,
>
> > > *an opinion* . . .

It then continues with a modifying phrase or clause:

> > . . . to $1,000 an ounce,
> > > *an opinion that is not shared by*
> > > *the rest of us.*

Topic: The idea that a sentence* comments on. It is what the sentence is about. The topic is usually the subject* of a sentence:

> *China* will eventually become a major industrial nation.

But the topic can appear in other constructions:

> *In regard to China,* it will eventually become. . . .
>
> *I believe that China* will eventually become. . . .
>
> *There is general agreement as to China's* eventually becoming a major industrial nation.

Transitive Verb: A verb* with a direct object*. The object can be made the subject* of a passive* verb:

> We   *read*   the book.
>
> The book   *was read*   by us.

By this definition, the verbs *resemble, become, stand* (as in *He stands ten feet tall)* are not transitive verbs.

Verb: Verbs have four forms:
    Infinitive: The "bare," or base, form of the verb: *go, be, have.* In many cases, the infinitive form follows a *to:* He wants *to leave.*

Finite: The verb inflected for present or past: *went, was, were, has, does, sees*. There is no difference between the infinitive and finite forms when the finite form refers to the present and does not have a third-person-*s:*

I *see* the book.

I want to *see* the book.

You can always identify the main verb in a clause* because it is also the finite form of the verb. To find out which word that is, just change the time the clause refers to. If the clause refers to the past, change it to refer to the present; if to the present, change it to the past; if to the future, to either past or present. The word you have to change is the finite verb:

He *decided* to leave.	He *decides* to leave.
He *left*.	He *leaves*.

The two other forms are the perfect and the progressive forms. Most English verbs use the *-ed* form for the perfect:

He has walk*ed;* I have danc*ed;* you have stumbl*ed*.

But many verbs have irregular forms:

She has s*u*ng; they were beat*en;* we have g*o*ne.

The progressive form always ends in *-ing:*

They were danc*ing,* walk*ing,* and sing*ing*.

Some Possible Revisions to the Exercises

Few of these exercises have a single correct answer: A good many of your answers will be different from but as good as those here; indeed, I would be surprised if many were not better. Trust your ear. If you decide your version is better than the answer here, try to state why: Don't depend on generalities like clarity and precision. Try to say *why* it's clearer and more precise: Is it shorter? Is it more specific? If your answers are less compact and direct than those suggested here, try to decide whether the difference between your version and mine is a significant difference. There comes a point in every sentence where another five minutes spent looking for the most concise and specific version possible is simply not worth the result. It's the first five minutes that count.

Exercise 1–1

1. We expected to establish new tolerance levels.
3. The governing committee announced that they would submit their report by the deadline.
5. The governor must refuse the request.
7. At that time, independent investigators measured the half-life of thorium more accurately.
9. The business sector did not independently analyze what caused the trade deficit. (did not attempt to analyze why trade was in the red)
11. Management was uneasy over the result of the survey.
13. The insurer must check the discrepancy in the data.
15. The police immediately investigated the affair.

17. After the last report, we studied the same principles of bilateral symmetry.
19. I believe that the administrators should consult with the student body before anyone changes the rules.
21. They must redetermine what personnel they need before local sources can assist them.
23. I would oversimplify the problem if I argued that all government officials administered their programs inefficiently.
25. Although social scientists have been developing ways to corrobate that their respondents have responded reliably and validly, Jones did not employ any of them in this study; as a result, we cannot rely on his respondents' exaggerated estimates of their situations.

Exercise 1–2

1. Depending on the rhetorical situation and the interests of the readers, the agents of *reanalyze* and *announce* might or might not be important.
3. Trotsky abandons his usual impassioned narrative style and puts in its place a cautious and scholarly treatment of theories of conspiracy (and instead, treats theories of conspiracy in a cautious and scholarly way). But the moment he picks up his narrative line again, he invests his prose. . . .
5. Almost certainly, we would want to know who has been ignoring the wiretapping regulation: For many years federal, state, and local law enforcement agencies (individuals?) have been regularly ignoring wiretapping restrictions.
7. We have written these technical directives as simply as possible because we are attempting to communicate more effectively with relatively uneducated employees whom we have hired in accordance with guidelines imposed on us by the federal government.
9. The researchers evaluated tissue rejection according to procedures that most other researchers have abandoned because those procedures consistently overestimated values for the production of antibodies (because those procedures consistently led them to overestimate values for . . .).

Exercise 1–3

1. The committee on standards for plant safety discussed recent announcements of regulations regarding air quality.
3. Phenomena involving the pancreatic gland are regulated chiefly by cells in the parasympathetic nervous system.
5. On the basis of these principles, we may now attempt to formulate rules by which we extract information from narratives.
7. The Federal Trade Commission is responsible for enforcing federal guidelines in regard to the durability of tires on new cars.
9. The Social Security program guarantees a standard floor for monthly income for individuals whose package of potential benefits is determined by what those individuals have contributed over the course of their lives.
11. Because state law supervises the organization of corporations (how corporations are organized), the federal government is unable to effectively implement measures that would reduce pollution.
13. On November 1, 1979, the secretary of the Department of Energy announced in a press release that after the Department of Energy and major manufacturers met on October 28 to discuss the matter, the manufacturers decided to dispose of their surplus stock of alcohol.
15. In order to interpret cardiac sounds, one must know intimately cardiac physiology and the pathophysiology of cardiac disease.

Exercise 2–1

1. This kind of stylistic criticism has two modes: analytic and normative. The analytic critic assumes that the best possible text is the one before him, and that his only task is to explain why the text is as it is. On the other hand, the normative critic assumes that the writer could have missed his intention and then explains where the writer failed to match his language to

his ideas. Which form of criticism we choose is determined more by the fame or obscurity of an author than by the intrinsic quality of a text.

3. Except in those areas continually covered with ice or scorched by continual heat, the earth is covered with vegetation. Plants grow not only in richly fertilized plains and river valleys but at the edge of perpetual snow in high mountains, not only in and around lakes and swamps but under the ocean and next to it. They survive in the cracks of busy city sidewalks as well as in barren rocks. Vegetation covered the earth before we existed and will cover the earth after evolution swallows us up.

Exercise 2–2

There are many possible answers to this problem. Here are only a few.

1. The people of this village hear something from the cathedral at Chartres which I do not; but it is important to understand that I hear something from this cathedral which they cannot. Perhaps they respond in awe to (this makes the villagers the agents of the action) . . . ; Perhaps the power of the spires, the glory of the windows strike them (this makes the topic the power of the spires, etc., but keeps *power* . . . as the seeming agent), but God has made Himself known to them longer than to me. . . . I recoil in terror from the slippery bottomless well (this makes Baldwin the agent of the action); the slippery bottomless well . . . terrifies me (this makes the well and the gargoyles the topic of the sentence but keeps them as the agents of the action). I doubt that the devil ever occurs to the villagers when the cathedral faces them . . . because they have never identified themselves with the devil/because the devil has never been identified with them. . . .
But the status which I derive from myth in the West imposes itself on me before the myth will change.

Exercise 3–1

1. The most important event in Thucydides' *History of the Peloponnesian War* was the catastrophic Sicilian Invasion.
3. In large American colleges and universities, teachers have limited opportunity to work with individual students. Or: the opportunity to work with individual students is limited.
5. Before a Board of Trustees may dismiss a tenured faculty member for cause, it must provide him with a statement of specific charges and prove that he grossly violated academic responsibility.

Exercise 3–2

1. Along with the aforementioned summary, we present studies that evaluate the reconstruction of upper and lower eyelids.
3. Clearly, in some parts of our country, overbuilding of suburban housing has recently led to extensive flooding and economic disaster.
5. Under these conditions, fuel lines and steam-heating systems in older coaches have also become frozen.
7. At about this time an event occured that would change the course of the war and of world history.
9. To start a dialogue, you can most usefully focus on real community issues rather than talk about broad problems.
11. DuPage County, sixteen miles west of the Loop and covering 338 square miles, has the fastest growing population in the region.

Exercise 3–3

1. During the reign of Queen Elizabeth, a popular story was that of King Lear and his three daughters (or for an audience who is entirely familiar with *King Lear:* the story of King Lear and his three daughters was a popular story). By the time Elizabeth died, it was available in a dozen easily accessible books. But most of these stories were simple narratives that stated rather

obvious morals and that failed to develop the characters. Several versions of this story must have been known to Shakespeare when he began work on *Lear,* one of his greatest tragedies. But while he based his characters on the stock figures of the legend, he turned them into credible human beings with complex motives.

3. We can explain this kind of severe condition by the hypothesis that the vibrio elaborates a toxin which alters mucosal and vascular permeability. In favor of this hypothesis are changes in small capillaries located near the basal surface of the epithelial cells and the appearance of numerous micro-vesicles in the cytoplasm of the mucosal cells. We believe that altered capillary permeability allows fluid to be hydrodynamically transported into the interstitial tissue and then through the mucosa into the lumen of the gut.

Exercise 4–1

1. The agencies that assist participants in our programs have reversed their recently announced policy to return to their original one.
3. Science depends on accurate data if it is to offer ideas that will allow mankind to advance safely.
5. Most patients at public clinics probably accept general medical treatment because their problems are rather minor and can be treated with understanding and attention.

Exercise 4–2

1. Graduate students looking for good teaching jobs face an uncertain future.
3. When investors believe that inflation will continue to grow, they usually invest in works of art.
5. The most important problem is how much the characters disguise the social tensions in the playwright's society.

7. Teachers have long been interested in how we memorize what we read. The first problem is to identify what features texts do and do not share; the second is to evaluate (measure?) what a person remembers from a text.

Exercise 4–3

1. But TV programming will probably continue to appeal to our most prurient interests.
3. The person we call Shakespeare could be someone else, perhaps even royalty.
5. Finally, China is on the verge of a major industrial expansion.
7. I do not believe that unexplored parts of the world have snakes larger than those we already know about.
9. Imagism mimics the haiku's strong visual patterns to provoke feeling while it simultaneously rejects the idea that particular feelings correspond to particular images.

Exercise 4–4

1. Inflation will continue if the federal government keeps on spending.
3. Scientists disagree whether the universe is open or closed, a dispute they will resolve only when they have computed the total mass of the universe with an error of no more than 5 percent.
5. We must develop tar sand, oil shale, and coal as sources of fuel, because we must make ourselves invulnerable to foreign powers that at any moment might cut off our oil.
7. We can treat cancer effectively only if we remove the tumor before it metastasizes.
9. When elections deal with those issues that normally escape attention, they will serve their intended function.
11. Stop taking the medicine only if you are still dizzy and nauseated six hours after you started taking it.
13. You will be prohibited from participating in the cost-sharing education programs only after you have had a hearing into why you were rejected.

Exercise 4–5

1. When we look at advertising systematically, we logically begin by defining the term. This establishes a shared point of reference that lets us approach the topic objectively. Unfortunately, because we must define advertising in so many ways, it makes it likely that we will be subjective. That indicates that we must examine popular notions about advertising carefully.

Exercise 5–1

1. Your car may have something wrong with one of its parts—the support plate that connects the front suspension to the frame. If the plate fails, you may not be able to steer your car, especially if it fails when you are braking hard. Also, we may have to adjust the catch that holds the hood down, because the secondary catch may be out of line. If it is out of line and the main catch is not secured, your hood could fly up. If the hood flies up, you will not be able to see in front of you. If either the support plate fails or your hood flies up, you could have an accident.

3. (a) By the words "damages because of bodily injury by accident or disease including death at any time resulting therefrom" we mean this: (1) What it costs to care for the injured person and the value of services that the injured or dead person cannot provide because of the injury or death; (2) the cost of damages that arise when an injured person brings suit against someone we insure, because the injured person is (a) employed by the insured person and (b) injured while working for the insured person.

   (b) If you are a policy holder, we will start to pay you or the Bank, as irrevocable creditor-beneficiary, under these conditions: You are insured by us, you are completely disabled by sickness or injury, and you cannot do any part of any paying job for more than thirty consecutive days.

   We will compute how much we will pay you as follows: Beginning on the thirty-first day you are disabled, we will pay you for every day you are still disabled according to. . . . We will continue to pay you for any

one disability for eighteen months. If you recover sufficiently for us to end payments and then you are disabled
again by the same cause, we will compute the period we
will pay you as follows: If you are disabled from the same
cause within six months after you recovered, we will
compute the remaining period we will pay you by sub-
tracting the first period of payments from eighteen
months. We will then pay you, as long as you are disabled, for the rest of the eighteen months.

Exercise 5–2

1. Highschool dropouts will usually choose to watch Lawrence
   Welk over Masterpiece Theater.
3. Go to the movies tonight and you won't sleep when you get
   home.
5. Because the corner gas station isn't open on Sundays any
   more, your neighbors may spend August in their backyard.
7. The guy who tightens a bolt every ten seconds on the line at
   Ford is less interested in another twenty-five cents an hour
   than he is in a job that he can enjoy.

Exercise 6–1

1. Responding to the problems we identified in our self-study,
   this college has already created many activities that meet the
   expanding needs and interests of our students. These new programs also reflect the traditional goals of the college: the
   liberal education of the whole person.
3. It is true that because responsibility is unclearly defined in this
   organization, its training program has a long history of financial problems and disputes among management. But it is
   equally true that in the last few years it has placed approximately half of its trainees in jobs equal to their abilities.
5. The soaring cost of energy has especially burdened those who
   can least afford it—the sick, the elderly, those on fixed in-

comes—all those who can least endure the hardship of lower temperatures. Consequently, we must create a program that would identify such people and then subsidize their fuel costs.

7. Nothing more severely challenges our belief in free speech than the Nazi party of America when it conducts marches and rallies Jewish communities. These American Nazis want only to enrage those who suffered most from German naziism in order to create a violence that will publicize their party and thereby attract more members and more money.

9. In this procedure, we assume the following: (1) We have a sample large enough to include the variation found in the total population; (2) we analyze the data according to accepted statistical procedures; (3) we can replicate the study under conditions the same as those of similar studies.

Exercise 7–1

The answers are only exemplary, of course.

1. Many school systems are returning to the basics, basics that have been too long ignored . . . a change that will be welcomed by parents everywhere . . . reasserting the old values that have been ignored for too long.

3. Why we age is a matter that has puzzled humanity for millennia, a matter that is just now being unraveled . . . a mystery that is just now being unraveled . . . inspiring questions that go to the heart of the human condition.

5. The recent fertilization of an embryo in a test tube has raised ethical issues that are troubling both scientists and laypeople, issues that go to the very center of how we define life and humanity . . . an event that will influence both religious and scientific thinking.

7. In 1961, the U.S. government announced that it would put the first man on the moon, a decision that proved to be one of the best we ever made.

9. In the 1960s, the Supreme Court ruled that anyone arested for a crime had to be given the widest benefit of legal doubt, a view not shared by the law enforcement officers who had to deal with crime more directly.

11. Systematic skepticism denies that we can ever know reality so long as it is screened by human perception, perception that changes reality before we can even begin to contemplate it or even to think about it . . . a point of view that denies both the accuracy of our senses and the intelligence of our minds.

13. During the Renaissance, affluent and politically stable scientists allowed streams of thought to flow together, streams of thought that had both political consequences for every government and intellectual consequences for every European culture . . . a development that changed not only the future but the past as well.

Exercise 7–2

1. Because Congress failed to anticipate the cost of inflation when it originally voted funds for the Interstate Highway System, the system has run into insoluble problems, problems that could spell the end of the most extensive construction project in world history.

3. Because TV game shows appeal to the cupidity in us all, they are just about the most popular daytime TV, a fact that does not bode well for evening TV.

5. Working with devices that can accelerate particles almost to the speed of light, researchers in high-energy physics are exploring the ultimate nature of matter, providing us with ever more puzzling facts about the basis of physical existence.

7. If before the next congressional election the government does not provide all political candidates with campaign funds, only the rich will be able to seek public office in numbers large enough to assure a wide selection of candidates, numbers that will not, however, include a wide range of political views.

9. In the last half century medical science has learned to detect and even to anticipate diseases that would formerly have appeared in our midst and devastated whole populations; it can now predict the outbreak of diseases such as influenza a year in advance, allowing us to prepare for their onslaught.

Exercise 7–3

1. They submitted an ecological impact statement identical to that of the previous year, so it will again be difficult for us to evaluate their data, because we still have no information independently verifying what they supplied.
3. Because we have reorganized the division for marketing research, information more accurate than that which we have received in the past should allow us to identify populations different from those we have traditionally aimed at. This information will be relatively easy to analyze because we have already accumulated demographic data such as average income, spending patterns, etc., for many different markets. As a result, we may expect an operation more efficient than that which we conducted last year.

Exercise 7–4

1. The new barbarians display a range of expressiveness to aesthetic experience that usually takes the form of "Wow."
3. With little sense of scholarly bias, historians impose on the past not just their private view of historical relevancy but the implied view of their whole social matrix.
5. The next point is the isolation of various clotting mechanisms in higher mammals.
7. It is universally acknowledged that when Woodrow Wilson refused to take into his confidence the leadership of the United States Senate, he caused the defeat of the Treaty of Versailles.
9. Last year in England, though, there was discovered a virus that bears no known relation to any other form of protein-based life.
11. Because we were unfamiliar with the mechanism, we were not able to detect any metal with it.
13. Because the students realized that the undergraduate curriculum had to be revised in the next few weeks, they put proposals on the agenda that had been discussed earlier.

Exercise 8-1

1. Those who keep silent over the loss of small freedoms will eventually find themselves being kept silent by the loss of large ones.
3. We should pay more attention to those politicians who tell us how to risk making what we have better than to those who tell us how to keep whatever we have from getting worse.
5. Too many teachers mistake neat papers rehashing conventional ideas for careful logic supporting unexpected truths.
7. Never mistake a style that is too difficult to penetrate for ideas that are too complex to understand.
9. This report does not adequately balance the importance of our immediate cash flow against the need to increase the size of our funded reserves.

Exercise 8-2

1. Few tendencies in our government have changed American life more than the unrestricted power of federal agencies.
3. The day is past when boards of education can expect taxpayers to automatically go along with the decisions of extravagant administrators.
5. If we invest our sweat in these projects, we must not seem to be working out of self-interest.
7. Throughout history, science has advanced because dedicated scientists have overcome the hostility of an uninformed public.

Exercise 8-4

1. The figures in the first quarter report point to some important facts about productivity, especially how hidden costs are forcing us to cut back our research budget. They reveal how much we need even more research into ways to stop the spiralling wages of unskilled labor.

3. We should not too devoutly hope that because we are rational we can make empty space part of our vision of the universe and of our place in it. We will fail because our animal nature prevents us from fully accepting the fact that we are mortal in a transient existence.

Exercise 10–1

1. From all available evidence no black man had ever set foot in this tiny Swiss village before I came. I was told before arriving that I would probably be a "sight" for the village; I took this to mean that people of my complexion were rarely seen in Switzerland, and also that city people are always something of a "sight" outside of the city. It did not occur to me—possibly because I am an American—that there could be people anywhere who had never seen a Negro.

   It is a fact that cannot be explained on the basis of the inaccessibility of the village. The village is very high, but it is only four hours from Milan and three hours from Lausanne. It is true that it is virtually unknown. Few people making plans for a holiday would elect to come here. On the other hand, the villagers are able, presumably, to come and go as they please—which they do: to another town at the foot of the mountain, with population of approximately five thousand, the nearest place to see a movie or go to the bank. In the village there is no movie house, no bank, no library, no theater; very few radios, one jeep, one station wagon; and at the moment, one typewriter, mine, an invention which the woman next door to me here had never seen. There are about six hundred people living here, all Catholic—I conclude this from the fact that the Catholic church is open all year round, whereas the Protestant chapel, set off on a hill a little removed from the village, is open only in the summertime when the tourists arrive. There are four or five hotels, all closed now, and four or five bistros, of which, however, only two do any business during the winter. These two do not do a great deal, for life in the village seems to end around nine or ten o'clock. There are a few stores, butcher, baker, *épicerie,* a hardware store, and a money-changer—who cannot change travelers' checks, but must send them down to the bank, an operation which takes two or three days. There is something called the Ballet Hall, closed in the winter and used for God knows what, certainly not ballet, during the summer. There seems to be only one schoolhouse in the village, and this for the quite young children.

Finally, there should grow the most austere of all mental qualities; I mean the sense for style. It is an aesthetic sense, based on admiration for the direct attainment of a foreseen end, simply and without waste. Style in art, style in literature, style in science, style in logic, style in practical execution have fundamentally the same aesthetic qualities, namely, attainment and restraint. The love of a subject in itself and for itself, where it is not the sleepy pleasure of pacing a mental quarter-deck, is the love of style as manifested in that study. Here we are brought back to the position from which we started, the utility of education. Style, in its finest sense, is the last acquirement of the educated mind; it is also the most useful. It pervades the whole being. The administrator with a sense for style hates waste; the engineer with a sense for style economizes his material; the artisan with a sense for style prefers good work. Style is the ultimate morality of mind.

ALFRED NORTH WHITEHEAD
THE AIMS OF EDUCATION

INDEX